Praise for

Dying On Purpose

How My Near-Death Experience Can Change Your Life

"Richard Steinhoff's story of discovery of his life's purpose through a near death experience is a fascinating encounter with a Heavenly being, teaching that we all have a distinct purpose for being here to serve humanity. His inventory of life questions and actions to fulfill your purpose will help anyone wishing to complete their mission here on Earth."
~ Brian Goodell, Olympic Gold Medalist,
Realtor, Motivational Speaker, Elected Official

"If you want more out of life, then you need to read "Dying On Purpose." Richard used his own experiences to put together a clever blueprint on how you can live your life On-Purpose and experience exceptional happiness and fulfillment. It is pure genius!
~ Daniel Hall, Host of the Real Fast Results Podcast at www.realfastresults.com

"In "Dying On Purpose," the author takes you on a journey that shows you how he turned his life around after a near-death experience. He then shares how you can change your life and make a difference. Brilliant!"
~ Genesis Milan

"Dying On Purpose" is a brilliant treatise on how the author's near- death experience changed his life, and how you can benefit from this experience to change your life. Everyone on the planet should read this book."
~ Kristine Weatherly, CFO, Spectrum Mechanical

"Richard Steinhoff does a beautiful job of relating to his reader. His near-death experience and the subsequent discovery of his life purpose is profound. The story leaves you contemplating your own purpose. Well done Richard. You too should read this book."
~ Lynette Montoya, CEO, Global Hotel Partners

"*Dying On Purpose*" *is a gem. The author shares how his high-stress lifestyle as a Realtor landed him in the hospital, where he had complications and almost died. His revelations about love, family, and legacy are brilliant and make you look at your life with different lenses. The book also provides the reader with sections on how they can figure out their own legacy and purpose. I would recommend this book to anyone who wants to learn how to live life to the fullest."

~ Linda Hollander, Author of Corporate Sponsorship in 3 Easy Steps, CEO of Sponsor Concierge, and founder of the Sponsors Secrets Seminar.

"*By sharing his journey with us, Richard not only has managed to capture the very essence of the questions we all ask ourselves but gently guides us in answering some of life's harder questions so we can lead a better life.*"

~ Lisa Dale, CEO, Seabreeze Management Company, Inc

"*In Richard's new book, "Dying On Purpose", he chronicles his transition from living Off-Purpose to living a purposeful life. He then shares with the reader how they can do the same. He is a genius. If you want to change your life and make a difference, you have to read this book.*"

~ Terry Goldfarb / RGP

"If you're not satisfied with your current life, this book is for you. "Dying on Purpose" will help you find a new life, one with purpose and filled with complete happiness and contentment."

~ Tom Antion, founder, Internet Marketing Training Center of Virginia, www.imtcva.org

"Rich Steinhoff his led a fascinating life – from years working on the Apollo program to running one of America's most successful real estate offices. He really knows how to get things done. Yet he points out, vividly, that success can come with a price. His description of his near-death experience and recovery was excellent."

~ Maralys Wills, Author, "HigherThan Eagles."

"Richard has sent men to space! Still, it took a near-death experience to wake him up to the beauty of his life and the need to live On-Purpose. His story is and is an inspiring tale from despair to hope to find one's calling. Thanks, Richard, for the guidelines and exercises, too."

~ Ellen Rohr, President, Bare Bones Biz, Inc

"Richard Steinhoff had it all—a beautiful home, a loving wife, a successful career in real estate, and a best-selling book titled Turning Myths into Money: An Insider's Guide to Winning the Real Estate Game. When a diseased gall bladder landed him in the hospital and a series of complications nearly killed him, Rich was reminded that his life, while full of motion, was empty of purpose. Immediately, he set about to discover his purpose and, once he had regained his health, to fulfill that purpose by writing a book to share the all-important message that true meaning and lasting joy in life come from serving others. In Dying On Purpose, he uses a series of carefully crafted questions to guide readers on a journey of self-examination and personal discovery toward a life lived On-Purpose."

~ Sherri Butterfield, writer and editor

DYING
ON PURPOSE

How My Near-Death Experience
Can Change Your Life

H. RICHARD STEINHOFF

Dying on Purpose: How My Near-Death Experience Can Change Your Life
© 2017 H. Richard Steinhoff. All rights reserved.

No part of this publication may be reproduced or transmitted in any form or by any means, chemical or electronic, including photocopying and recording, or by any information storage and retrieval system, without permission in writing from Author or Publisher (except by a reviewer, who may quote brief passages and/or show brief video clips in a review.)

Disclaimer: The Publisher and the Author make no representations and warranties with respect to the accuracy or completeness of the contents of this work and specifically disclaim all warranties, including without limitation warranties of fitness for a particular purpose. No warranty may be created or extended by sales or promotional materials. The advice and strategies contained herein may not be suitable for every situation. This work is sold with the understanding that the Author and Publisher are not engaged in rendering legal, coaching, psychological, accounting, or other professional services. If professional assistance is required, the services of a competent professional person should be sought. Neither the Publisher nor the Author shall be liable for damages arising herefrom. The fact that an organization or website is referred to in this work as a citation and/or a potential source of further information does not mean that the Author or the Publisher endorses the information the organization or website may provide or recommendations it may make. Further, readers should be aware that Internet websites listed in this work may have changed or disappeared between the time this work was written and when it was read.

Some names and identifying details have been changed and some of the story lines have been recreated.

Published in the USA by:
H. Richard Steinhoff

Printed in the United States of America
ISBN   978-1-7322852-0-0 (paperback)
           978-1-7322852-1-7 (e-book)

Cover and Interior Design by Darlene Swanson • www.van-garde.com

To Elaine,

my wife, my life partner, my rock,

and my love, I dedicate this book.

You have provided inspiration, love,

and support, for which I am truly grateful.

Without you, I would not even be here.

Acknowledgements

First and foremost I want to thank Jared Rosen for your support and incisive advice. Your creativity is on a different level than most people. You brought out something in me I didn't even know was there, and the result was spectacular. Thank you, Jared.

Next, I want to thank Chris Van Buren for generating a creative marketing plan for my book. You, sir, are a genius. It is a great pleasure to work with you and watch your mind create things others could not even imagine.

I want to thank Laurie Gibson for her creative editing and her intuitive suggestions that made my book better than I imagined. Thank you Laurie for a job well done, as usual.

I also want to thank my entire family for their support and encouragement, not only just on this project, but for my entire life. Thank you Elaine, Lisa, Brian, Sydney, Rick, Mary Anne, Brittany, Michael, Ryan, Nina, Kevin, Cameron, Hailey, Hannah, Gabe, Debbie, Jerry, Kaitlyn, Jasmine, Tonia, Chris, Josue, and Diana. I love you all.

Thanks to everyone who provided endorsements. You are all very special to me, and I am truly grateful.

Foreword

When invited to write the Foreword for this book I felt honored and grateful to contribute. This book (and its author) is an expression of love. Rich's book, and the experiences he shares with you in every chapter, is truly exceptional. His story demonstrates that we have choices. He chose to pay attention to how he was living his life and how he was not living his life. In one experience, Rich chose to return to his body, as you'll read about in his out-of-body near-death experience, and share how it lead to him discovering his purpose and how he now lives his life On-Purpose. He is inviting you to find your purpose and fulfill it every single day. When you do, you will live a life of joy and contentment.

Many people go through life not realizing that we have been given the gift of choice. It is now time to grab hold of the reins of your life and direct it where you want to go; do what you want to do and be who you want to be.

For most of my young life, I thought I was dealt the card of a difficult life. In all sincerity, I assumed that I was meant to struggle. It is not a happy way to live: completely blind to the fact that we can choose new decisions, different decisions that can change the trajectory of our life.

When I was nineteen, I met a man, who would change my life for the better. He spoke of a life filled with possibilities and promise. You must understand that prior to meeting Bob Proctor all I knew, lived and breathed was negativity. I was raised in a hostile, destructive and abusive environment. Because of being a negative person, my results reflected that mindset. The concept that we could create a phenomenal life was not even on my radar of consciousness.

Fortunately, though I decided that the way I was living my life was not enjoyable and felt that there must be a better way. To go from a life of misery to a life of fulfillment was a stretch in my imagination. But, when I invested the time and energy to study human potential, I discovered that I was destined for greatness.

And, so are you!

That may seem unfathomable at this moment to imagine that you are destined for greatness, and yet you are. We all are. Dive into this unique book, become captivated and discover from Rich's life experience that you can and must live your life On- Purpose.

And, enjoy the journey- because life is meant to be fun.

~ Peggy McColl, President, Dynamic Destinies
and *New York Times* best- selling author

When you are inspired by some great purpose, some extraordinary project, all your thoughts break their bonds; your mind transcends limitations, your consciousness expands in every direction, and you find yourself in a new, great and wonderful world. Dominant forces, faculties and talents become alive, and you discover yourself to be a greater person by far than you ever dreamed yourself to be.

~ Patanjali

Contents

	Prologue xvii
Chapter 1:	When We Go Off-Purpose 1
Chapter 2:	My Not-So-Real Life 11
Chapter 3:	A Message from the Light 29
Chapter 4:	Transformed By the Near-Death Experience (NDE) 41
Chapter 5:	Re-entry 71
Chapter 6:	Reboot Your Life 81
	Epilogue 195
	About the Author 199
	Bonus Gift 203
Appendix A:	List of Values 205

There are two great days in a person's life – the day we are born, and the day we discover why.
~ William Barclay

Prologue

If you died today, could you say you lived your life On-Purpose?
Would you feel a sense of fulfillment in your life?
Would you have any regrets?
Would you be ready to leave this world?
Well, I am going help you with these answers by taking you on a journey with me and sharing my experiences with you. The journey is about my quest to find my life's purpose. It will start where I realized I was living a life Off-Purpose and my struggle to overcome that problem. We will endure heartache, health challenges, and job changes along the way.
During this journey, I succumbed to stress and ended up in the hospital with a very bad diagnosis. During my stay, my heart stopped and I had an

out-of-body experience where I encountered a heavenly body. This experience changed my life. I was told to return to my body because I had not yet completed my purpose on Earth.

And, at the end of this journey, I found my life's purpose, as you will see.

Then I will teach you the questions you need to ask yourself to find your true calling, so that you, too, can live your life On-Purpose.

Come along with me and see what the possibilities are for you. My goal is to help you find your purpose so you can live a happy, fulfilled life.

Everyone in this world was put here for a purpose. If you don't know yours, you need to read this book.

To your success,

H. Richard Steinhoff

http://www.hrichardsteinhoff.com/

Man's here for the sake of others.
— Albert Einstein

Chapter 1: When We Go Off Purpose

Are you excited about what you do?

Do you experience joy every day?

Do you wake up and can't wait to get started with your day?

If not, you are living your life Off-Purpose.

You really don't want to be there because you will never be happy, and life will feel like a struggle. Living life Off-Purpose is stressful and many times leads to health issues. This happened to me and led to an extraordinary Near-Death Experience. While I was undergoing surgery for a life-threatening illness, I awoke and noticed a brilliant white light in the hallway. I arose to investigate the light and as I moved toward it, I realized I was floating and all my pain had vanished. Then a large, super-natural being appeared. He seemed to be glowing from within. He started to communicate with me without speaking. His message was, "You must return to your body, you have not yet completed your purpose on Earth."

I remember looking at my motionless body and thinking, I must leave my Off-Purpose life behind and start living On-Purpose.

Living Off-Purpose, you never feel fully alive because you believe your presence on this planet does not make a difference. You are not concerned about what your legacy will be and what your obituary will say. For many people, living a good life, being kind, and loving as deeply as possible are enough. But, if you really love yourself and want to be kind to yourself, you will pursue your dreams fearlessly with passion and vision. Then you will feel that your life is on a purposeful trajectory.

If my words resonate with you, then sharing my journey of becoming On-Purpose may inspire you to take the actions you need to awaken your highest aspirations.

Launching a Career

Since my childhood, I had been fascinated by airplanes. One day, my dad took me to the airport, where I saw my first airplane in person. And I remember thinking, *How can such a large object fly through the air?* Right then I was hooked. I started building model airplanes. At first, I made small gliders from balsa wood, a very lightweight wood, and the planes were easy to fly. Every boy in the early 50's had a balsa wood airplane, but my fascination with airplanes did not end there.

Over the next few years, I built dozens of planes and eventually graduated to models with gas engines and remote controls. The largest one I built had a wingspan of over six feet. I became quite expert at flying these models, and, at this point, my big dream was to design and build real airplanes when I grew up.

When I eventually got to college, I studied aeronautical engineering and business. Thinking that I would get a job with a large airplane manufacturer, I exceeded my expectations and secured a job working for an aerospace defense contractor on the Apollo space program. I was drawn to aerospace because it was a step beyond my childhood dream to build airplanes. My work contributed to building space vehicles that flew out of the atmosphere (and eventually to the moon).

When I was looking at my first airplane with my dad, I wanted so badly to build airplanes. I never imagined I would be building space vehicles. It was exhilarating. Imagine, putting a man on the moon! That was President Kennedy's dream, and it became the dream of everyone associated with the Apollo program. President Kennedy was an inspiring, dynamic leader and mastermind of the space program. How often can you go a step beyond your big dream?

I was so fortunate.

It was very exciting and challenging to work on the space program. I was interacting on a daily basis with some of the world's brightest minds. My company designed and built the Lunar Excursion Module (LM).

We were excited about the upcoming launch of Apollo 13, which we had been working on for more than a year. During that time there were many design changes, but at this point we believed we had the best design possible. Several of us traveled to Cape Canaveral in Florida for the launch. Our plane arrived in Orlando late in the afternoon, and we rented a car to drive to Cocoa Beach, where we checked into our hotel, ate dinner, and went to bed early.

We got up the next morning, drove to the Cape for the launch and went into the Command and Control building. It was April 11, 1970. Just prior to liftoff, we went outside to the VIP grandstand for a better view of the launch, which was absolutely spectacular. The sound of the giant Saturn V rocket was deafening. The ground was shaking so much it felt like an earthquake. Also, the giant fireball created by the liftoff was breathtaking. We watched the ascent until Apollo 13 disappeared into the atmosphere.

I felt a sense of pride to have been a small part of this,

and also to be an American. I truly wish that everyone in the United States could have witnessed this launch. It would have made you feel great to be an American and would have instilled pride in you as well.

We were scheduled to be at the Cape for only two days after the launch, but on the second evening we heard over the loudspeaker the chilling words, "Houston, we have a problem," Apparently, an oxygen tank had exploded. The reason he said Houston is that Mission Control was in Houston and Launch Control was at the Cape, where we were. The next three days were action-packed. The crew chief had to move the astronauts into our Lunar Excursion Module for their safety. He and his staff then had to figure out how to rig an air filter so the astronauts could breathe clean air and stay alive. As you know, they were successful. Apollo 13, with its crew intact, landed safely back on Earth on April 17, six days after it had taken off.

Years later, I was fortunate enough to meet Captain Jim Lovell, commander of Apollo 13. He was very gracious and thanked me for being a part of the Apollo 13 team.

After Apollo, I transferred to the Space Shuttle program, where I worked for the program's chief engineer. This, too, was a challenging program. One big issue was the ceramic tiles on the underside of the fuselage. They kept falling off, which was a critical problem because these tiles prevented the ship from burning up when reentering the atmosphere. Our engineers labored around the clock to find a solution. We kept trying different adhesives, but none of them seemed to work.

Finally, one of our engineers came up with a formula that looked promising. It tested well, so we used it on a real ship, the *Columbia*.

We all crossed our fingers as it launched into space. When *Columbia*'s mission was completed, and it started its return journey to Earth, we drove to Edwards Air Force Base (about a hundred miles north of Los Angeles) for the landing and to check out the tiles. *Columbia* reentered the atmosphere and converted to an airplane for the landing.

We watched it land, and *Columbia* then taxied to the designated inspection area so our engineers could check it out. To our amazement, the new adhesive had worked. Only fifteen tiles came off, and it happened during liftoff. Everyone was relieved. We could now go home.

Back Here on Earth

By then, it was 1981. I was no longer feeling the excitement that was prevalent throughout my involvement in the space program. We had accomplished some major goals, but I could see the handwriting on the wall. The space program looked like it was going to be winding down in the near future. We were missing the dynamic leadership of President John Kennedy, and there was no one to take his place.

My passion was also gone. My childhood dream had faded. Plus, my inner voice was saying, *"You have another purpose in life."* I decided to follow my instincts, so I said goodbye to an industry that had been an important part of my life for a very long time.

I was now faced with the task of determining what I should do next, so I started looking at many different options. You know what I am talking about; I'm sure you've had the same experience of having to change jobs at some point in your career.

So, even though part of my dream was lost, I had to move on. Whatever I decided to do, I had to replace the income I had earned in aerospace to support my lifestyle. I also wanted to do something I would enjoy. I thought I would just concentrate on high-income opportunities.

Then one day I was talking to my friend Carol, who was a Realtor. She suggested I obtain a real estate broker's license because she thought I could be really good at the job.

She said, "Hey, you are a college-educated Mensa member, don't you think you could figure out how to make a killing in real estate?"

"A killing? Do you really think so?"

"Yes, I do. You are good with people; they will trust you because you are honest."

I like real estate, and I like people.

So, I signed up to take the California real estate broker's license exam. They call it the "Mini Bar" because it lasts all day, eight hours, and has a high failure rate. I also enrolled in a license prep course. The requirements for taking the brokers exam included having a bachelor's degree or higher, and taking six college-level real estate courses, which I had done.

Even back then, the universe was giving me signals that my life was Off-Purpose. I remember driving through smog-shrouded downtown Los Angeles on my way to take a real estate license prep course. As I was driving down Wilshire Boulevard, I saw a 747 airliner in the distance, heading toward LAX and I got a sinking feeling in the pit of my stomach. I thought, *Where am I going? What am I doing here?* Even though I was happy that I had fulfilled my dream in aerospace, I was still apprehensive about the future. Then I looked up and saw a beautiful high-rise condominium building. It was magnificent. So I thought, Maybe real estate wouldn't be so bad. I could make a lot of money by helping others attain their goals. Not too shabby.

The company's office was across the street from the California Department of Real Estate, and for four weeks I spent one day each week in Los Angeles, taking practice exams. Finally, the day came to take the real exam. I left home early to ensure I wouldn't be late. During the drive, my thoughts went back to my time in aerospace. Did I make a mistake by leaving? Was it really that bad?

I was brought back to reality when the traffic came to an abrupt halt. I finally found a parking spot and headed to the DRE. After taking a seat in the exam room, the Department of Real Estate monitor gave us instructions on how to take the exam.

As he droned on, I started chewing on my pencil. Then I thought, *What in the hell am I doing here? What have I done? I am here taking a test so I can sell something to someone? I know real estate is a noble profession, but how will I be On-Purpose?*

After answering seemingly endless questions from students about the test we were about to take, the monitor finally distributed the exam.

Seeing the actual test for the first time, I was delighted that I had spent the money to take the exam prep course. I remember sitting there looking at the clock while taking the test and thinking, Is this going to be my life? I'm not sure I am doing the right thing. Even though they gave us four hours, I was finished with the test in ninety minutes. I went across the street to the prep company office.

They gave me more practice questions to take

during the lunch hour. Right before one o'clock, I went back across the street to the DRE testing room. The afternoon session started exactly at one o'clock. I suppressed all the negative thoughts I had about the future and just concentrated on the test at hand. I finished the test an hour and a half later, turned in my paper, and left for home, confident that I had passed the test, but feeling like I might have made a wrong turn down a one-way street in my life.

Find a purpose in life so big it will challenge every capacity to be at your best.
– David McCoy

Chapter 2:
My Not-So-Real Life

Now, I had the task of determining where to work. With the help of my friend Carol, I researched local real estate offices. Then, I interviewed with the brokers of the four offices we thought would be the best fit. After these interviews, I said to her, "There is no way I can work for these people."

I had just come from an industry with intelligent, well–educated, creative people. It was the total opposite of the in-your-face, in-the-trenches world of real estate. Be assured; I am not knocking real estate agents, they are just a product of a "here today, gone tomorrow" industry mindset.

But I was used to an entirely different approach to attaining goals – a long-term, strategic approach that assured integrity and patience. In the space program, people's lives depended on the quality of our work. The world of real estate put me in shock. I was disillusioned and missing the excitement of aerospace. I remember watching John Kennedy speak and becoming so inspired that nothing seemed impossible—not even putting a man on the moon. Everyone in the program shared a vision of leaving Earth and traveling into space. All of us who worked there had a common goal and would do whatever was necessary to make that happen. We were like soul mates, sharing thoughts and feelings.

This is in direct contrast to real estate, where the participants have no common goals, and each agent's individual goal was making money. There was no incentive to help each other. I was now 45 years old and very disillusioned.

"What can I do now?" I asked Carol.

"You have a broker's license, why don't you start your own office?" she replied.

"What?"

"Yes, I mean it. You can start small. Rent a small office and hire a few agents to work for you."

I thought about what she said. "Do you really think I can do that?"

"Yes, you can. I will be with you every step of the way," she replied.

So, with trepidation, we rented a small office, hired

four agents, and purchased an ERA Real Estate franchise. We were off and running and not sure where the race would end. The anxiety I felt at that moment was a mix between the excitement of achievement and the terror of achieving something that I sensed would never bring me inner fulfillment.

That night, lying in bed, I started to think back to my childhood. In addition to designing airplanes, my other dream was to be a major league baseball player. That dream was shot down early; I realized being a major league baseball player was not a job you could find in the help-wanted section of the newspaper. I guess these are the dreams we call pipe dreams.

Sometimes, life gets in your way, and sometimes you listen to the wrong people, and sometimes you take many detours. To find out if this has happened to you, just look behind you because your dreams have taken the back seat.

While I was in high school, I worked in my uncle's grocery store. He wanted me to take over the store after I graduated. But that was his dream, not mine. I wanted to play baseball and build airplanes. Sometimes, other people's dreams can hijack our dreams. To earn enough money for college, I had to continue to work after high school, so I ran my uncle's store, but I was very clear that this was not going to be my life.

Some people just take the easy road. For them,

security and consistency outweigh any existential quest. We all have different paths in life with different purposes. Most people want freedom in life, and I contented myself with the idea that real estate could give me the freedom to explore more of life's roads.

The High Road to the Crash

After a few years, our real estate office became very successful. Our company was in the top 100 out of 4,500 ERA Real Estate offices nationwide. Because business was good, I decided to purchase a new Cadillac El Dorado. At the time, It was the car of choice for real estate agents because of its size and luxurious features, and it was very comfortable for clients.

It was at this time when I met my future wife, Elaine, at a California Real Estate Convention in San Diego. When I first saw her across the room, I was immediately attracted to her, so I asked her to dance. Once I held her in my arms, there was a magical connection and sparks flew. We started dating and were married a year later. (She would become my anchor in life.)

The Orange County real estate market was booming because the economy was expanding and people had jobs. It was so hot that when a Realtor previewed a new listing, so many real estate agents would attend, that it caused a major traffic jam in the area, and you had to park blocks away from the property. Also, most new listings had multiple offers the day they came on the market. I have seen as many as fifty offers on a single property.

In those days, 1987, we usually presented offers in person because there was no fax or Internet available. Since there were usually multiple offers, the seller would schedule offer presentations one after the other. The Realtors would show up for the presentation with their buyer in the car. Each Realtor would then present their offer in turn. The reason why buyers were in the car is so that they could sign counter-offers on the spot. This was very important to the success of the purchase because the seller would go to the next buyer if your buyer wasn't immediately available to execute the transaction.

It was nuts! Because of this, along with other things, real estate was a very stressful environment.

By the way, the homes usually sold for more than full price. The Realtors had to engage in a guessing game as to how high the other Realtor's buyers were willing to go. (Real estate had turned into an art form.) The secret to winning in these multiple-offer situations was convincing the seller that your buyer would perform and close the sale. This was important because many unqualified buyers were writing offers in that crazy market. I had become an expert in this technique, and with the help of another special technique, I never lost a sale involving multiple counter offers.

Obtaining listings in that market was also a challenge. When someone wanted to sell their home, they called four or five agents from different offices to come over and do a listing presentation. Then they would decide who they wanted to work with.

Sometimes agents would try to buy the listing by telling the seller they could get a much higher price than the current market value of the home. In our market, sellers were pretty sophisticated and rarely fell for that pitch.

One day, I received a call from Mrs. Terry. She asked me if I would be interested in listing their home; she and her husband were moving to Arizona. I asked her if they were talking to any other agents and she said they were going to talk to five agents. In this situation, you like to be the last one to present, because the seller wouldn't list with anyone until they have heard them all. If you are last, you have the opportunity to close on the spot. I asked her if I could be last, but she wouldn't commit to that, so I made an appointment for the next day. I went over the next day and gave my best presentation explaining why they should list with me. I thanked them for their time and left.

Two days later, I received another call from Mrs. Terry. She said they had decided to list with me, so I went right over to their home. After they had signed all the papers, I asked her why they decided on me. She stunned me by saying they had seen me drive up in a brand new Cadillac and figured I must be a very successful agent.

(So much for ego.)

Almost anyone who wanted to buy a house could do it because lenders had loosened their qualification requirements. I became concerned about that situation because people were getting loans with payments they couldn't afford. It was a recipe for disaster. As it turns out, I was right, but I take no pleasure in that.

Then the stress of running an office started to take a toll on my health. My appointment book looked like a blotter, with appointments canceled, appointments changed, and new appointments every week. My head was always spinning. I found myself managing an office with a cast of characters who definitely didn't think like engineers.

People like Joy. She was an attractive, slender young woman with dark hair. She was very pleasant, but she always talked using her hands. One day, I went on a listing appointment with her, as I frequently did with new agents. We were driving along the 91 freeway in Orange County, and she was at the wheel. Then her cell phone rang, and I thought, *Oh no!* She picked up her phone in one hand and immediately started talking using her other hand. I remember thinking, *Who is steering the car?*

I looked over at her. We were going seventy-five miles per hour, and she was steering with her knees! So, I said a little prayer. Fortunately, the call did not last long, and both of her hands returned to the wheel.

Then there was Peter, who wanted to manage everyone else but couldn't manage himself. He was an engineer with a full-time job and worked for us part-time. We thought he would do well because he was so intelligent. However, all the time he spent in the office was devoted to telling other agents what they should be doing. He would dole out advice to any agent who had the misfortune of being there at the same time as Peter.

One day, I called him into my office and told him we were letting him go. He was shocked. "How can you let me go? I am your top agent," he said.

I replied, "You have been here one year, and you have had no listings and no sales."

"How can that be?" he said in disbelief.

I showed him his sales chart.

"You are good at telling other agents what to do, but you don't do those things yourself. We just cannot afford to support you any longer."

He left the office that day, still not understanding why.

Fred was also an interesting case. He was young and, as it turned out, lazy. His live-in girlfriend had a good-paying job, so he didn't really have to work if he didn't want to. Apparently, he didn't want to. Each time

I called him, he was at home watching TV, instead of being in the office prospecting for clients. After six months of this, I called him into the office to let him go. Just like Peter, he was shocked. He really had no clue.

Cindy, a new agent, created a different experience for us. She called me into the conference room one day where she was meeting with clients. She introduced me to them, and the husband explained they had just driven to Orange County from Las Vegas, where he was a professional gambler. They wanted to buy a condo in Irvine. They had selected one of the properties Cindy had shown them. He asked, "How much is this condo?"

So I looked at Cindy, and she said, ""One hundred and fifty thousand."

He replied, "O.K." He reached into his jacket, pulled out a roll of bills, counted out $150,000, and said, "How soon can we move in?"

I spent the entire weekend holding $150,000 in cash, hoping not to get robbed.

All these agents were real people, but the only purpose we shared in common was making money, and that felt empty to me.

At that point, we had thirty-five of them, and I was forced to use the "Sand Bucket Management", jokingly defined as running around all day with a bucket of sand in each hand, putting out fires. One day I was driving to another part of town to show some property, grabbing a McDonald's hamburger on the way. This is known as a Realtor's lunch: grab and go, eat in the car. I stashed the wrapper under the seat and opened all the windows so my client wouldn't smell the food. I was stressed because I was running late and had to wolf down lunch. Also, I can't tell you the number of times when I came home at nine or ten o'clock at night, often without dinner. Not very good for family life. But it didn't matter because I had to do it to put real estate deals together. It was killing me, but such is the life of a Realtor.

Realtors had to be on the job 24/7 because clients were usually available for looking at property or for signing documents during the evening or on weekends. During weekdays, Realtors had all their other tasks to do, like handle escrows, process paperwork, negotiate sales, write contracts, preview listings, conduct market research, prospect for clients, and many more. The pressure caused by this created a very stressful environment.

Broken Down by Stress

During my appointment I developed a sharp pain in my abdomen that didn't go away, so after we finished, I went to the doctor. After examining me and running some tests, he told me that I had Gastrointestinal Reflux Disease (GIRD), and put me on medication to ease the pain. He also told me to reduce the stress in my life, which was a major cause of my problem. (Like that was going to happen!) My diet had to be restricted to reduce the acid in my stomach. No spicy food, tomatoes, fried food, coffee, or alcohol. This was going to be a mega lifestyle change for me. (No McDonalds, either.)

He also told me I had asthma. Lately I noticed I was out of breath a lot. Now I knew why. The doctor put me on several medications to relieve the symptoms. He also told me that both conditions were made worse by stress.

Our average sales price was about $500,000, creating a commission of $30,000 for the office. Every time a deal had a problem, the pressure to fix it took a toll on me. The stress would cause me to get short of breath or develop acid reflux pain. (Sometimes the pain was so intense, it would feel like a heart attack.) Problems would occur like having a buyer who couldn't qualify for a loan or a seller who wouldn't make the necessary repairs.

If a deal fell apart, I would have to be concerned about paying the office rent as well as my mortgage that month. This is an example of chronic stress, as opposed to acute stress.

Acute stress is a response to a temporary situation. We all do this; it's the flight or fight instinct that had helped us to survive. But chronic stress is present every day. It just keeps whittling away, whittling away, and whittling away, till you crack or have a major health issue.

The condition of my body was a read-out of my health. It was like a meter, showing where I was over the line. The acid reflux, asthma, and physical exhaustion were all reflections of my living Off-Purpose.

That's when I decided to take an inventory of my life. It was pretty clear to me that I was not living my life On-Purpose, and if I continued on this path, my body would exit me from this world. I was not doing what I was born to do.

Yet, I still did not know what that was. I did know I was totally stressed out, and that was a big part of being Off-Purpose. Also, having health issues, being unhappy, feeling unfulfilled, and having life be a struggle are all part of it as well. And I experienced all of these. At this point, I had been in real estate about 15 years.

What woke me up was the effect stress was having on my health. I did some research on the effects of stress on the body. According to WebMD, 43 percent of all adults in America suffer adverse health effects from stress. And that over 75 percent of all doctor visits are for stress-related illnesses. Additionally, they stated that stress was a big factor in health conditions like obesity, headaches, heart problems, high blood pressure, diabetes, asthma, arthritis, fatigue, stomach problems, sleep disorders, and depression. I fit right into this group. How many people do you know who struggle with some of these illnesses?

Also, during my research, I found out that people who were living their life's purpose were mostly happy, healthy, and free of stress. Maybe that was the answer. If I could discover my purpose, then I could do something about my health and turn my life around. I knew I couldn't go back to aerospace. That part of my life had ended. But it seemed like I was trying to seek fulfillment through the challenge of making money. Even though my dream was no longer building airplanes or playing baseball, I was still doing something that would bring joy and happiness to other people's lives by helping them to fulfill their real estate goals and make money in the process.

And that made me think; *I may be earning a living, but is my life fulfilling?*

Living Off-Purpose was starting to raise a red flag in my life.

The Big Shock

When the 2008 recession hit, it was a shock to millions of homeowners. Suddenly, the real estate market fell off a cliff. Homeowners had been given loans with no income verification and with their rock-bottom FICO scores. And, most of these loans had an adjustable interest rate that converted to a high fixed-rate in five years. Many of these loans also had low down payments, sometimes as little as 5 percent. The banks had a nickname for them: NINJA loans. No Income-No Joke.

The major problem came when banks packaged all their questionable loans, called subprime loans, into mortgage-backed securities and sold them to Wall Street. Then, when homeowners couldn't make their mortgage payments, the mortgage-backed securities became worthless. The ripple effect was so big that many large lending institutions failed and the government had to bail them out. My premonition had become a reality. The United States went into a full-blown recession, and we took a lot of other countries down with us. I suggest you watch the movie "The Big Short," to get a better picture of what was happening in real estate at this time.

The total loss of equity in pension funds and real estate values was over $5.5 trillion. Because of the 40 percent drop in home prices, homeowners found themselves owing more on their loan than their property was worth. It was known as being "underwater," because you were drowning in debt; you couldn't breathe. It was very stressful and painful.

At one time, they were an estimated 17 million homes underwater. Home foreclosures became rampant, and a new program called the "short sale" came into prominence. A short sale occurred when the homeowner sold their house for less than they owed on their mortgage. Between 2008 and 2015, over 16 million homes were foreclosed upon. The market was flooded with REO's (Real Estate Owned bank properties). As a result, home prices plummeted. At the same time, home sales went in the tank, partly due to tightened lending practices and partly due to income loss. This affected the entire economy because thousands of related businesses like electrical, plumbing, framing, plastering, roofing, lighting, home improvements, appliances, and, of course, home building, were also affected. (Economists say residential real estate is a multiplier of seven, that is, for every dollar not spent by homebuyers, seven dollars would not be spent at related businesses.)

The banks had now gone from being loose to being almost impossible with lending. Instead of giving a loan to anyone who could fog a mirror, they went to the other extreme. It was almost like they wouldn't give someone a loan unless the borrower had enough money in the bank to pay cash for the house. I am being facetious, but their lending practices had become absurd.

Realtors were also adversely affected, and the ranks of licensed professionals were decimated. Entire offices were going out of business. Typically, 90 percent of real estate sales are done by 10 percent of the agents. That makes it very tough for most agents to survive when sales are hard to come by. So, thousands of Realtors dropped out of real estate to find jobs with a steady paycheck.

I would drive down the street and notice that the employee parking lots at Macy's and Wal-Mart were filled with Mercedes and Lexus, probably belonging to former Realtors who were now working retail. It is tough enough to live a commission-based lifestyle in a good economy, but this was ridiculous. People could not go six or eight months without a paycheck. That's when I realized I was in a boom-or-bust industry. Definitely not very good for avoiding stress.

The Search Begins

Sometimes, shock can lead the way to finding your purpose. As a result of the housing crisis and its aftermath, I went on a quest to find my life's purpose. I read every book I could find on discovering your purpose, from "*The Happiness of Pursuit,*" to "*Have You Seen My Sexy? A Woman's Guide to Finding Purpose,*" and studied all the various techniques. I tried every one of them and, by doing that it became clear to me what I needed to do.

Until then, I had been helping people one at a time. I now realized that I could help thousands of people nationwide by putting all my real estate knowledge into a *book*. I could help homeowners facing foreclosure; buyers facing obstacles in purchasing a home (including difficulty obtaining financing); people who would like to invest in real estate for their future; and people who needed a good, competent Realtor. Plus, I could do it at a national level.

So, I started writing a book. I was very fortunate to find a publisher who was as excited about the book as I was. My book, *Turning Myths Into Money, An Insider's Guide to Winning the Real Estate Game,* went to the top of Amazon's New Releases list within thirty days of being published.

In no time, I became a nationally known real estate expert. I was a featured guest on dozens of radio talk shows from coast to coast, along with several television news programs, including two appearances on Fox Evening News in Los Angeles. In addition, I was a featured speaker at the National Association of Realtors Annual Convention and was appointed an Honorary Member for Life by the California Association of Realtors.

My dream of helping homeowners nationwide had become a reality.

You are here in order to enable the world to live more amply, with greater vision, with a fine spirit of hope and achievement. You are here to enrich the world.
~ Woodrow Wilson

Chapter 3:
A Message from the Light

Though my book seemed to be helping thousands of people, I was not helping myself. Something was still missing. I didn't have a feeling of fulfillment like I should have when you are living your life On-Purpose. Plus, the stress of running a business was starting to whittle away at my health again. I could feel parts of my body becoming tight, like a rubber band ready to snap.

Sometimes, it felt like my mind was going to snap, also. My health was falling off a cliff, just like the real estate market. Then, one day I became very sick. I felt like I was going to throw up every meal I had eaten during the last year, plus, I had a stabbing pain in my abdomen. I called my primary care doctor, Dr. Barton, and he sent me straight to the emergency room.

Trip to the E.R.

My wife, Elaine, drove me to the hospital. As we were driving, I looked at the mountains in the distance, thinking how much I loved Elaine, and how fortunate I was to have her as my wife. She is a gem. We had been married twelve years. During that time, she was always at my side, supporting me through good times and bad. We had a "magical" relationship, and I really didn't want to die and leave her now.

We arrived at the hospital and went into the emergency room. I was shocked! There were people everywhere, even some sitting on the floor. I thought I should get attention first because I might die any minute. There were lots of people ahead of me who had minor cuts and scrapes, and I really didn't want to wait for them.

Fortunately, my doctor had called ahead, and I actually didn't have to wait long. By that point, my pain level had reached eleven out of ten. It was excruciating! I felt like I was going to pass out any second, but I didn't want to because I might not wake up. They put me on a gurney in a cubicle cordoned off with plastic curtains. The nurse was there, and hooked me up to an IV, took my vital signs, and tried to comfort me.

"We're very busy. It might be a while before the

doctor can see you," she said.

I asked how long she thought it would be. She told me about an hour or so.

The curtains did not provide much privacy. I could hear a child screaming while having a wound stitched up. I could hear someone else vomiting, and someone else begging for drugs. It was chaos.

If you have ever been in an E.R., you know what I mean. As I was lying there, I had an intuitive sense that I was about to embark on a journey into a realm I never even think about, and I had no idea where I would end up. It was like *Alice in Wonderland*, and I was about to go down the rabbit hole.

I looked at my cell phone. And then my phone went dead, and I had this strange feeling that some people coming into the E.R. for small things also end up dead.

The doctor arrived thirty minutes later.

"My name is Dr. Frederick. What's the problem? Where does it hurt?"

"The pain's right here in my abdomen," I replied.

"We are going to run some tests to find out what's wrong," he said as he pressed on my abdomen. "I'll see you when the tests are completed."

Soon after he left, an intern arrived to take me to the first test, and I was off to the races. For the next four hours, I was shoved into MRI tubes, loaded onto X-Ray tables, stood in front of nuclear scan machines, squashed with an ultrasound scanner, and poked with needles for blood draws.

Everything was done with such urgency that I was starting to become concerned. I was thinking, *Is this it? Am I going to die now? Wait a second, what will I die from? Is it my stomach? They haven't told me anything.*

Then the morphine kicked in, and my concerns began to disappear, one-by-one, like bubbles on a head of beer.

After the tests were finished, I was returned to my cubicle in the E.R.

He Had a Lot of Gall

Dr. Frederick came back a little while later.

"We have determined that your problem is a badly infected gallbladder. The good news is, it can be corrected by removing it surgically. However, we have to put you on heavy doses of antibiotics for twenty-four hours before we can operate."

"Don't I need a gallbladder?"

"No, your body can function just fine without one."

I remember thinking at that time, What does a gallbladder really do?

Because I now had a couple dozen hours of free time, I decided to do a little research on gallbladders using my i-Pad. Did you know the gallbladder is an organ located on the right side of your abdomen whose primary function is to store bile, a digestive enzyme produced by the liver? The gallbladder releases bile into the intestine, where it helps to digest fat.

This was news to me. Apparently, there are no long-term effects from losing your gallbladder. In this situation, the bile would drip continuously from your liver directly into your intestine at a very slow rate, so there is no disruption in the digestion of fat. I was thinking, *Maybe I don't have a lot of gall now, but soon I will have no gall at all because they are removing my gallbladder.*

When Dr. Frederick told me about the surgery, I thought, *Great, twenty-four hours in the E.R. My poor wife.* I had sent Elaine to the hospital cafeteria to get something to eat. When she returned, I told her about the surgery and encouraged her to go home.

"I don't want to leave you alone," she said.

"I'll be fine. I want you to get some rest, so I don't have to worry about you. Go home!"

To my joy, she did. But then I had a feeling of emptiness because my lifeline was gone. So there I was, lying there in the E.R. with nothing to do. When you have nothing to do, your mind wanders, and you think of things outside of your current environment. This could be a really great thing, especially if you're in a hospital. Think of a place that's really special to you – somewhere

where you are at peace and without stress, like lying on the beach, listening to the sound of waves.

My place is on the patio at our desert house, lying in a lounge chair, looking at the deep blue, cloud-free sky, and listening to the calming sound of the waterfall in the lake just below. It makes me want to drift deeper into this relaxation state.

I was jolted back to reality by the buzz of my iPhone.(The nurse has been kind enough to charge it for me.) It was a text from Elaine.

"Good night, sweetheart. Sleep tight. I love you."

I didn't get much sleep. Every two hours the night nurse checked my vital signs and gave me pain medication every four hours. Did I mention that I wasn't allowed to eat or drink? Everything had to come through the IV. I started thinking, *How did I get here? Am I not living my life On-Purpose? Why am I so stressed?*

I couldn't answer those questions.

My Rock of Gibraltar

The next morning at ten o'clock, Elaine called to check on me. She said she would be there at one o'clock. She asked me if I needed anything.

"No, just you," I replied.

After hanging up, I felt a wave of relief because I would see her soon. She was—and is-- my Rock of

Gibraltar, always there for me. That's what keeps me going. She always makes me feel that everything will be all right. I knew she would not let anything bad happen to me. Everyone should have someone like that.

I'm thinking, *Six o'clock (surgery time) is so far away, but I knew Elaine would help me pass the hours.* When she arrived, she told me there was a sign outside my cubicle that said, "No food or liquids." We talked for hours, mostly about our children and grandchildren, and were interrupted several times by nurses and nurse's aides.

When you are feeling awful, all you want to do is just lie there and sleep, but in a hospital they are constantly monitoring your vital signs, taking blood, and bothering you all night. My stress level was not much lower as I was now stressed about being in the hospital and missing work.

When you are in the hospital, the greatest joy is having visits from people other than the doctors, nurses, dieticians and other clinicians. So I was truly delighted when my daughter Lisa showed up with her husband and our granddaughter, thirteen-year-old Sydney, who is always good medicine for me. It is pretty impossible not to feel joy when she is around. After a way too short time, the interns arrived to take me to surgery. "I'll see you in a little while," I said as they wheeled me off to the operating room.

The O.R. is a sterile place. Everything is stark white;

everyone wore green gowns, masks, and little hats. And gloves. I noticed it was also cold. As I looked around the room from my gurney I was fascinated by all the high-tech equipment, wondering how much of it was being used for me. The surgeon, Dr. Carman, was there. "We are going to remove your gallbladder by laparoscopic surgery," he said. (Laparoscopic surgery uses a lighted microscopic camera. They make four small incisions for the camera and surgical instruments. This produces less scarring and promotes a faster recovery.) He continued, "It should take about ninety minutes. Do you have any questions?"

I had none, but the thought occurred to me, *What if I didn't make it through the surgery*? Wow! I really did not want to go there and think about the ramifications.

There were a lot of other people in the room, and I wondered why they were all there. One of them came over to me.

"I am your anesthesiologist. I am going to give you something to put you sleep," he said. And it did.

My Near-Death Experience

When I finally opened my eyes, I saw a foreign world. Everything was pure white, unlike anything I had ever seen before. There was a kind of light that radiated from within everything. At the end of the hall, the light was so bright that I arose out of bed to see where the light was coming from. Then, I noticed I wasn't walking; I was floating. Also, all the pain in my body had vanished, and I had a feeling of calmness like I've never had before. In that eternal moment, I knew deep inside that everything was whole and I was whole regardless of whether or not I had a gallbladder.

That's when a large being appeared to me – an apparition that seemed to be glowing with a brilliant white light from within. Even though the light was brilliantly bright, I was not blinded by it, which puzzled me. All I could see was his head, radiating this super-bright white light. He was looking at me directly and shaking his head. It felt like he could see directly into my soul. He didn't appear to have a body. It was all pure white below his head. I couldn't tell if he had clothes or a robe because he had no shape.

"Who is that? Where am I? Did I die?"

So many questions were racing through my mind.

Then he pointed to my bed, so I looked back and saw my motionless body lying there.

"Are you kidding me? This can't be happening."

Without speaking, he started communicating with me. I could clearly understand him, though his lips weren't moving. Thought transfer, I said to myself.

He spoke these words, and a chill rushed through my body: "You are not dead. You still have much to do with your life. You must return to your body; you have not yet completed your purpose on Earth."

I wanted to know more.

"Who are you? Where am I? What is my purpose?"

He seemed to sense my thoughts.

"It will all be explained to you in good time."

"Will I see you again?" I asked.

"Yes, when you have completed your journey."

So I reluctantly turned to look at my body, thinking, *How do I get back in?*

The next thing I know, I felt someone shaking me, and I heard a voice off in the distance. The voice grew louder, "Mr. Steinhoff, wake up."

I opened my eyes and saw a nurse.

"What time is it, and where am I?"

"You are in the recovery room, and it is midnight," she replied.

"Midnight! I went into surgery at six o'clock. What happened?"

"They had a little trouble. Do you need something for pain?"

I noticed that all my pain had returned and I was no longer calm. "Yes, please."

I began to reflect back on what had just happened. *Was it a dream or did I really leave my body? Did I actually die? Why? The Being must have aided my return to my body because I don't remember re-entering it.* Before I could deliberate further, the pain medication kicked in, and I dozed off. It was about two thirty in the morning before I was taken to a real room in the Intensive Care Unit.

Elaine was waiting for me. She looked tired and very worried. But she told me I did great and that everything was going to be all right.

I believed her. After all, she was my rock. Little did she know how important that would be in the days ahead. I wanted to tell her about my experience, but I couldn't find the words. It was indescribable in our world.

I told her to go home and get some sleep, and asked where Lisa was. She told me Lisa had gone home.

I found out later what had happened. When Dr. Carman attempted to remove my gallbladder, it fell apart and spilled infectious bile into my abdominal cavity. He said I also went septic. Because of this, he had to cut me open immediately to save my life.

I'd also had another complication: I suddenly stopped breathing. They put me on a breathing machine and called my pulmonologist, Dr. Darcy, who immediately came to the hospital. They finished the operation with me using a breathing machine.

Unfortunately, Elaine had seen Dr. Darcy running down the hall at the same time a "Code Blue" announcement came over the loudspeaker. Code Blue is the call for emergency help when a patient's heart stops.

By this time, Elaine was in a panic, thinking that the call might be for me. She'd been told the operation would take ninety minutes; at that point, it was well over three hours later. Finally, after four hours, Dr. Carman came out to talk to her. He told Elaine what had happened and that it didn't look good.

"We don't expect him to live through the night," he said. "I'm sorry."

That's when Elaine sent Lisa and everyone else home.

She didn't tell me any of this until twelve days later when I went home myself. Since nobody told me, it had never occurred to me that I could actually die.

The secret of happiness: Find something more important than you are and dedicate your life to it.
~ Daniel C. Bennett

Chapter 4: Transformed by the Near-Death Experience

Because of my very fragile condition, I would have to spend the next ten days in the hospital. It was Saturday; Dr. Carman came in at ten o'clock in the morning with a troubling message. "We have a minor problem," he said. "You have a bile leak, and we have to put a stent in to stop it."

"Does that mean I have to have another surgery?" I asked.

"Yes, but it won't take long."

Under the Knife Again

The only thing I could think of was how this would affect Elaine. She'd already been through hell. When she arrived a few hours later, I told her about the situation and the impending surgery.

My Rock said, "No problem. You are in good hands. The hospital will take good care of you, plus, you have the best surgeon." Where would I be without my Rock, and where would my Rock be without me?

Then a thought flashed through my head, *What if this was the last time I saw Elaine's face?* I quickly put that thought out of my mind.

It was about five o'clock when they wheeled me to the O.R. After the surgery, Dr. Carman came to see me in the recovery room. "You are going to need some time to recover; you are very sick," he said on his way out. Why would a doctor tell you that you're very sick? Of course, you are sick; you are in the hospital. What did he mean? Does he think I am not going to make it? Do all doctors use that phrase with dying patients? Then I remembered the words of Elaine's surgeon when she was in Intensive Care after her heart operation the year before.

"She is very sick," her doctor had said. "She is probably not going to make it. You should spend as much time with her as possible."

That triggered my brain. Dr. Carmen had used the exact same words. *So, am I going to die?*

I returned to my room around seven o'clock to see Elaine's smiling face. My saving grace was that Elaine was always at my side, smiling and upbeat. She again told me everything went well and that they were confident the leak had been stopped. I don't know how confident they really were; for the next five days, they ran daily tests to check for leakage. Even though she seemed upbeat, I could see the fear in Elaine's eyes. As I look back, I was trying to stay positive also, but my scientific training from college and my aerospace career kept filling my mind with worst-case scenarios. You know what I am talking about.

Elaine is a Realtor, and she was in the middle of a transaction when all this occurred. I found out later that she didn't want to leave me, so she had her clients meet her at the hospital to sign their transaction documents. She continued to handle the transaction throughout my hospital stay without missing a beat. Fortunately, her clients were empathetic and understanding.

Suddenly, an alarm went off. It startled me. It was coming from the machine with my IV lines. I didn't know what was happening. I thought, *Is there an air bubble in the line? Am I going to die? Will this malfunctioning machine kill me?* I reached for the cord with the call button, but it was tangled up with the IV line. I began to panic. The thought of being close to death was frightening. I still didn't know if my NDE was real or not, and I wasn't sure what would happen after I die. I did know I was not yet ready to die. I had a wonderful family, and I want to spend a lot of time with them before I went. Also, I had many items on my bucket list I wanted to accomplish.

Why can't I get the call button cord untangled so I can call the nurse? I didn't want this machine to cause my death. Then Elaine came out of nowhere and started untangling the cords. She finally reached the call button and pressed it. Kay, the weekend night nurse, was there in an instant and fixed the IV machine. She told me I had never been in danger because the machine shuts off automatically if there's a problem, so I shouldn't panic if it happens again. Good to know.

Elaine and I continued talking until nine o'clock when she left for home. After she had left, Kay returned to change my bandage.

"I want to see it!" I told her. This was the first time I'd been alert enough to check it out. When she removed the bandage, I was stunned to see a sixteen-inch scar crossing diagonally from my lower right abdomen to my upper left abdomen. A very neat row of staples held the skin together. It looked like a big zipper.

"Where's the handle for this zipper?" I asked.

"We keep it at the nurse's station," she said. "I'll be back in an hour with your pain meds."

At ten that evening, I received my daily text message from Elaine: "Night, night. Sleep tight. Love you."

Then Kay returned with my pain medication. I went out like a light. I barely remember her taking my vitals at two that morning.

On Sunday, Dr. Carman came in at his usual ten o'clock and told me he had to place a draining tube in my abdomen to remove the excess bile.

"It won't take long. I'll see you at one o'clock in the O.R."

Here we go again, the third day in a row. Maybe I should make a standing reservation for that operating room? I'd already decided to do everything the doctors recommended because they were the experts—and I wanted to get well and go home. I called Elaine to tell her about the operation. She planned to arrive at one o'clock and wait for me in my room.

Disclosure

As I lay in bed still obsessed with what had happened to me during my NDE, a bright-eyed young man came in and explained he was a respiratory therapist and he was going to give me a breathing treatment ordered by Dr. Darcy. He then hooked me up to a nebulizer machine, which sends a steroid vapor into the lungs. I put the tube in my mouth as he turned on the nebulizer. That is what started me thinking about breathing. If you stop breathing, you die. This took me back to my NDE. I wanted to ask my doctor about it, but he was a no-nonsense, fact-oriented individual and I was afraid he would think I was crazy. Because he was a surgeon, I also wondered how many times a patient had flatlined under his knife, and if any of them ever told him they'd had a near-death experience. I really did want to have a doctor confirm that my experience was real.

My son had brought me some books on NDE's. When I received these books, I realized, *Oh my God. All these books were written by doctors about their own near-death experiences.* The books were:

Promised by Heaven by Mary Helen Hensley

Proof of Heaven by Eben Alexander

Evidence of the Afterlife by Jeffery Long

Code Blue: A Doctor's View of His Own NDE by S.R. Carson

Between Now and Then by Richard House
To Heaven and Back by Mary Neal

I wanted to show Dr. Barton these books, but because I was afraid of what he might think, whenever he came into my room I would hide them under the sheets so he couldn't see them. But I still wanted to talk to someone because I questioned if my experience had been real.

Back to reality. I finished my breathing treatment and Judy, the weekend day nurse, showed up about fifteen minutes later—none too soon for me. My pain level was way up. Because she was wearing a cross pendant, I knew she was spiritual. I was thinking, *I'll bet she knows about NDE's.* When I asked her, she said, "Oh yeah. It happens all the time. I used to work in cardiac surgery. Many patients told me about their out-of-body experiences while I was there. We had situations that were unbelievable. Patients would remember conversations between doctors and nurses while they were unconscious and under sedation. Some also remembered events taking place during surgery while they were asleep. This made me a believer in Near-Death Experiences. There was this one lady, Karen, who came in with a heart attack and while we were performing bypass surgery in O.R., she flat lined. The doctors worked frantically to revive her, using everything they had, including paddles, but nothing seemed to be working. They were about to give up, so I said, 'Her husband and two little children were in the waiting room, and I, for one, am not ready to tell them they no longer had a wife and mother. We can't give up. Keep trying.' They kept working, and all of a sudden, I heard a cough. Then her heart monitor started beeping. I couldn't believe it; she was alive!

Later, in the recovery room, I talked to her and she startled me when she said, 'Thank you for not letting the doctors give up on me. What you said about my husband and children touched me deeply. I really wanted to come back to them, and you made it happen. Thank you from the bottom of my heart.'

"It then occurred to me that she must have left her body to be able to observe what was happening to her under anesthesia, so I asked her about it. She told me that she was floating above her body and then went into this tunnel of light, where she was told to return to her body. That's when she came back and observed what was happening in the operating room. She also didn't remember re-entering her body, but she was so thankful she had. Her husband and children were so happy, also. Great story! "

"Thank you for telling me" I replied.

They came to get me for the operating room at twelve thirty. When I got there, the anesthesiologist told me he was going to give me something to make me sleepy. The next thing I knew, I was back in recovery.

They told me I would be there about one hour. It was about three o'clock that afternoon when they wheeled me back to my room.

This time, I looked like a bionic man: I was connected to an oxygen tank through my nose, with a breathing tube down my throat, a large IV in my arm, and a tube protruding from my stomach that was connected to a pump with a storage tank.

Nonetheless, Elaine was beside me again, saying, "You did great. Now your belly can empty."

Judy came in to put something in my IV.

"What do you have today, chicken or beef?" I asked.

She giggled and told me it was pain medication. I thanked her.

I was very tired, so I dozed off. A little while later, I heard voices, seemingly off in the distance. When I opened my eyes, Lisa and Sydney were there. Yippee!

"Poppy, how are you feeling?" Sydney asked. She's called me Poppy since she was eighteen months old because she couldn't say Grandpa. I told her I was feeling great, now that she was here.

I looked at Lisa. She had a worried expression. She said they brought me a present: a Get Well Bunny. Then Sydney handed me a stuffed rabbit. I thanked them, and Lisa said they had to go.

"Bye, Poppy. Feel better."

After they had left, Elaine told me that because I

looked so bad, Lisa couldn't stand to see me like that, so she had to leave. That's why they didn't stay longer. Elaine stayed until eight that night and looked very tired when she left.

I waited for her text, and it came at ten o'clock: "Night sweetheart, see you in the AM. Love you."

I could now go to sleep myself.

Blood is Life

The lab technician woke me up at four in the morning to take some blood. I didn't go back to sleep because people kept coming in for different tests. I felt like a guinea pig, but I knew they had my best interests in mind.

Dr. Carman showed up around ten that morning and told me they were going to have to give me a blood transfusion because I had lost a lot of blood and I was anemic.

Yet another complication. Keep them coming; I can take it, I thought.

A short time later, Rachael, the weekday nurse, brought in two pints of blood. As she administered the transfusion, I thought about my blood and how precious it is, and how precious life is. And, that some unknown person's blood is now circulating in my veins. Even though I will never know who it was, I was still grateful to them for helping to save my life.

When Elaine arrived, I told her about the blood transfusion. She was stunned. She said the doctors hadn't told her about this. I told her I just found out at ten that morning. I still did not realize the seriousness of my condition, but apparently, she did.

Just then, a man wearing a white coat came in. He said his name was Dr. Jarbin, an internal medicine specialist at the hospital assigned to me and that he would be checking in on me daily and coordinating my care. He asked me if I had any questions.

I told him I had one: "When can I go home?" He said he couldn't answer that right now because I had a ways to go before I was well enough to go home and that he would check on me tomorrow. I thanked him as he left. Then it occurred me; I still had not had anything to eat! All they gave me was sugar water.

After Elaine left at eight o'clock, I suddenly felt very alone and very frightened. Then my phone buzzed. It was a text from Elaine:

"Sleep tight. Everything will be all right. Love you."

With that, my fears vanished. She always had that effect on me. Everyone should be so lucky. As I dozed off, I barely noticed Sandra, the weekday night nurse, checking my vital signs.

On Tuesday morning, I was surprised when Rachel brought in two more units of blood.

"What's this?" I asked.

Rachael told me the doctor had ordered more blood because two units weren't enough.

"Am I going to be all right?"

"Yes, you will be fine. This blood will fix you right up."

When Dr. Carman arrived, I asked him why I was getting so much blood. He said it was necessary because I was still anemic. He told me I was going to need some time to recover because I was still very sick.

(There it is again, I am still "very sick.")

I still had no clue as to how close to death I had come, and I wasn't really able to comprehend what had happened to me. As I was sitting there with an IV in one arm and Rachael pumping up the blood pressure cuff on my other arm, I started thinking about my near-death experience again and wondering what other people's experiences were.

NDE After-Effects

Since I wanted to find out about that and also make sense of my experience, I decided to do some research on Near-Death Experiences (NDE's) on my i-Pad. Here's what I discovered:

The first known NDE was documented by Plato in his dialog "*The Republic*" around 380 B.C.

The phrase "Near-Death Experience" first appeared

in a book by Dr. Raymond Moody published in 1975. There were so many near-death experiences occurring that a group of researchers founded the International Association for Near-Death Studies (IANDS) in 1981. Every day in America over 700 people have an NDE, with an estimated total of at least 12 million cases to date. I wanted to go deeper, but I was getting very tired, so I postponed further research.

My son Rick and his wife Mary Anne came to see me in the afternoon. It gave me a lift to see their smiling faces and to feel their support. My spirits were buoyed by their presence.

Rick told me I looked great.

"You need glasses," I said.

"Come on, you know you're going to beat this thing. Where is your optimism?"

I told him I had no doubt that I would; it's just tough getting there.

"That's the spirit," he told me.

I thanked him for the pep talk.

Then he asked me about the food, and I told him I hadn't been allowed to eat yet.

He said. "That's one way to diet." So I told him I want to lose weight, but this is not how I would like to do it.

With that, they had to leave.

"Get better fast," they said as they left.

When Elaine arrived at six o'clock, she started telling me how great I looked. She is truly amazing. I am so fortunate. Then I told her about the additional blood transfusion. She looked concerned, so I told her what the doctor had said about it being necessary for my recovery. Our conversation was interrupted yet again by the malfunctioning IV machine buzzer. This time, the nurse came in less than two minutes, much to our relief.

Elaine said she talked to all of our children every day, even though they were also coming to see me. Only our daughter Debbie, who lived outside of Ft. Worth, Texas, was unable to visit me. Everyone else did.

Elaine stayed until ten, and then departed to get some sleep. Then Sandra, the night nurse, brought my tray of assorted medications. I became very drowsy, but stayed awake long enough to see Elaine's text message: "Night, night. Love you."

On Wednesday morning, I awoke at four thirty and couldn't get back to sleep. A short time later, a technician came in to take my blood. This would become a routine part of my day.

Then, Dr. Darcy came in and told me I had fluid in my lungs, and they were going to give me a strong antibiotic through my IV to prevent pneumonia.

I ruminated, *The challenges keep coming, don't they?*

I dozed off for a while, and when I awoke, I felt

someone holding my hand. I looked up and saw our daughter Nina smiling at me. She asked how I was doing, so I told her I was doing better, I think, but it had been quite a ride. She said she and Elaine had been talking daily, and that she was so glad I was doing better.

"You had me scared for a while," she said.

"Sorry, it was out of my control. But I am optimistic now, so don't worry," I told her. She seemed satisfied with my answer.

We talked for about another hour; then she had to leave for an appointment. After Nina had left, I decided to do some more research. I opened my i-Pad to search NDE's and found out that many people develop an unusual sensitivity to light and sound after an NDE, which explains why, all of a sudden, I had those very same problems. (I never did like hard rock music very much, anyway.) I was always asking the nurse to turn down the lights, and I seemed very sensitive to loud noises. Another physiological change that occurs is a reversal of the body clock, which in my case, lowered my blood pressure. I had been taking 100mg of Cozaar daily for high blood pressure, and now I take 25mg every other day. Quite a difference.

Nearly everyone who has had an NDE loses their fear of death, which was the same for me, and over 98 percent of them believed in life after death. I have had a fear of death since childhood. I always knew I would die someday, and wondered what happened after death. *Is that it? Is it all over? Or is there something after your body dies?* I, along with millions of others who have experienced an NDE, now knew the answers to these questions. Yes, there is life after death. Your spirit lives on in a form we don't yet understand after your body dies. Even though I lost my fear of death, be assured that I would like to stay in this body as long as possible.

I still have a lot to do.

Also, I did not ever intend to get a divorce. I could not stand to live without my Rock. It is unthinkable. But here are some statistics on divorce rates you might find interesting. The national divorce rate in America is about 51 percent, but for people who have experienced an NDE, the rate is 65 percent. The higher divorce rate may be due to people re-evaluating their lives and finding out their spouse no longer fits in with their new life purpose. Divorce is kind of like a death in that you are moving into the unknown. Both of these events are very stressful.

As far as careers go, I was now planning to write books that help others find their way. This was sort of a career change for me. (Leaving a job is also similar to death because, again, you are moving into the unknown.) Interestingly, 75 percent of people who experience an NDE change careers. When they find out what they were meant to do, it is almost never what they are currently doing.

It is an amazing feeling when you finally figure that out.

On Thursday morning, Rachael brought in a technician who took me for several different tests. I asked them if there was an extra charge for additional stops, and they told me it was all part of the service. It is a good thing I had my pain medication before we left because my body was manipulated into positions that would normally be painful.

When I returned to my room, Rachael was there. She told me they were taking me for a walk because Dr. Carman said I needed some exercise to get well. She said she would be back at two thirty.

To my surprise, my son-in-law Brian came to see me around twelve thirty. I told him I was delighted to see him. He said he had a meeting close by so he thought he would stop in and see how I was doing. I asked Brian if he thought I looked well enough for Lisa to see me because I didn't want to scare her again. He said that I did and that they would come by during the weekend with Sydney.

I told him I was looking forward to it.

"See you this weekend," he said as he left.

At two thirty, Rachael came back to take me for a walk, with two assistants.

This should be interesting, I thought. I hadn't been on my feet for several days, and I was hooked up to so many devices, I felt like a spaceman. Rachael told me not to worry; they had it all covered.

So, the three of them proceeded to detach me from the oxygen tank, the drainage pump, etc., so that I could move around. Then, they got me out of bed and on my feet. I was very wobbly and unstable, but with one of them holding each arm, we started off down the hall. We were going very slowly; I asked Rachael to get a calendar so she could time me. (She laughed out loud.) I finally made it half-way around the hall, then I had to stop. I was totally exhausted, so they brought me a chair. After a ten-minute break, I had no choice but to navigate the other half of the hall to return to my room. They put me back in bed and hooked me up to all the various equipment again.

The Scientific Theories

As I was being re-connected, I realized that, in a way, we're all hooked up to the physical world just like I was hooked up to the IV's that were keeping me alive. But what is the physical world? Quantum physicists say that everything is energy. So, my connection to the physical world could be all in my mind. This started me looking into what had happened with my NDE. Was it a hallucination? Some scientists say that NDE's are just hallucinations. After researching the subject, here is what I discovered. Hallucinations are usually illogical, fleeting, and distort reality, whereas NDEs are orderly, logical, and clear. People tend to forget hallucinations, but NDE memories remain vivid for years. Also, NDE's lead to changes in personality, beliefs, and values, which never happens with hallucinations.

I went further to find out if there was another theory. That's when I discovered the scientific theory that NDE's are caused by oxygen deprivation in the brain. Further investigation revealed that oxygen deprivation in the brain produces chaotic hallucinations, confusion, and disorientation, and always take place while the person is awake and conscious. NDE's occur while the person is unconscious, usually with no brain activity. Also, doctors have compared heart attack survivor's oxygen levels for those who had an NDE with those who did not, and found virtually no difference.

Still wanting to know more, I discovered the Drug-Induced Theory that NDE's can be induced by specific drugs like Ketamine. I learned that researcher Karl Jansen studied Ketamine for twelve years and concluded that there is a soul independent of existence and that it persists after death. Ketamine cannot take you there.

I found one more theory that NDE's can be created by stimulating the temporal lobe of the brain. My research showed that there is no empirical evidence that stimulation can cause an NDE. The characteristic emotions resulting from temporal lobe stimulation are sadness, loneliness, and fear, as opposed to the NDE experience of calmness, peace, and love.

Some scientists claim that death is the end of consciousness. Their analogy is that it's like when you shut off a television set, and that ends the TV signal. The TV set is dead. Of course, this is not true. The TV signal is still there in the airwaves after you turn off the TV. Similarly, the human soul continues to exist after that person's body expires.

After reading all that, I was exhausted and fell asleep immediately.

I woke up just in time to see Elaine walk into the room. I also noticed my dinner was sitting there: jello and broth. (Believe me, I'm not complaining! At least it was real food, not the kind that comes through an IV.)

I told her about my experience in the hall, and she said she was very proud of me. We continue talking until about ten o' clock; then she went home. I waited for her text, which came about forty-five minutes later: "Night, night. See you tomorrow. Love you."

Picky-Picky-Picky

Friday morning, Dr. Carman came in at seven thirty and told me that we had a problem. I had developed two blood clots in my left leg. I asked him if that was dangerous. He said it was. They had to get rid of the clots before they traveled to my heart or lungs.

He said, "We're going to remove your IV line and replace it with a PICC line. At the same time, we have to put you on a blood thinner to dissolve the clots."

I asked what a PICC line was.

"It's an IV line placed deep in your left arm, so they don't have to keep changing it out." The nurses had been changing my IV line almost every other day. He said he would come back at ten thirty with a team of specialists.

Now, I had something else with which to be concerned. Suddenly, I had a sinking feeling in the pit of my stomach. I thought, I survived all of the previous surgeries only to die from a blood clot?

I was hesitant to tell Elaine because she had been through so much at this point. She didn't need one more thing to worry about, so I decided to tell her after it was over.

Dr. Carman arrived at ten thirty, along with a pair of nurses. After two tries, they were finally successful in installing the PICC line. It took about an hour. Also, they put motorized compression boots on both legs, which took some getting used to while trying to sleep. These kept pumping 24/7. He also told me I would be receiving shots of the blood thinner Heparin in my abdomen twice a day.

A little while later, my daughter-in-law, Mary Anne, walked in. I told her it was a nice surprise. She said she was on her lunch hour and thought she would look in on me. (She worked at the hospital in the biomedical laboratory.) I asked her if she had seen any interesting lab work on me, and she said she had not seen anything. We talked for a while; then she had to return to work.

"See you soon. Feel better."

I thanked her for checking on me.

After she left, my thoughts returned to the blood clots. I had made it through so many challenges, and was determined I would not let this problem get to me. I thought, *I need something to take my mind off of this.*

So, I went back to my i-Pad to do more NDE research. I located information on Veridical NDE's. This is where people having an out-of-body experience have observed things while they were unconscious that were later verified when the person regained consciousness. People have seen instruments being used and have recalled conversations between doctors while they were unconscious. This can only be explained by the person having had an out-of-body experience.

I had to stop my research because Rachael came in at

three o'clock to take me for a walk. This time, I made it all the way around the hall without stopping, even though it took almost forty-five minutes. After they had hooked me back up, I got out all my books on NDE's again. (I now had eight of them.) I had them spread out all over my bed and the tray next to it when Elaine came in.

"What is this?" she exclaimed. So I had to tell her about my NDE. She stared at me with a shocked expression. I am not sure she believed me. It truly is a hard thing to grasp. She did, however, ask me many questions about it. I told her I just could not stop reading about it because I wanted to know if my experience had been real. Our discussion was interrupted when my dinner arrived. I sent Elaine to the cafeteria to get something for herself. She brought it back so we could eat together. Not totally romantic, but at least we were together and alive to enjoy it.

We talked some more after dinner; then she left for home. I waited for my nightly text, which came at ten fifteen: "Night - night, I love you."

Then I crashed for the night. It had been a traumatic day.

On Saturday, Judy came in around seven with my medications and some good news: they were going to help me take a shower today. It had been ten days since I'd had one.

"Sounds great to me."

" See you at three," she replied.

I had no time for research that day. Judy and two aides came to take me to the shower at three. After my shower, they returned me to my room and hooked me up to all the devices that were keeping me alive

As I lay there, I heard something over the hospital loud speaker: "Code Blue, room 242, Code Blue, room 242." *Hey, that's my floor.* I was in the Cardiac Intensive Care Unit. I started thinking: *Is someone dying? That could have been me."* I felt so sorry for their relatives and hoped it would not happen to mine, especially Elaine.

Elaine returned around six that evening and we ate together, as she brought food from the cafeteria. (I was delighted to have cherry Jello!) We talked nonstop until nine when she headed for home.

I thoroughly enjoyed our nightly talks because it took my mind away from my health issues.

As usual, I waited for her nightly text. She normally sent it as she was going to bed. It came about ten thirty: "Night-night, love you, see you tomorrow."

Sugar Coated

It was Sunday, and this day had a very different start. Dr. Carman came in at seven thirty and told me my blood sugar had spiked to 161. He said they were going to give me insulin to get it under control. So I asked what had happened because I hadn't been eating anything with sugar.

He told me it was probably all the sugar water I had been drinking, and it was nothing to worry about.

That's easy for you to say.

After he left, Judy showed up with my insulin injection and also told me not to worry.

Why does everyone tell me not to worry? It's worrisome.

Dr. Jarbin then came in and told me that if they could get my blood sugar under control, I might be able to go home the next day.

"What? Are you serious?" I asked.

"Absolutely. You have made amazing progress. I see no reason why you can't be released tomorrow."

I was so excited to think that I might be home within twenty-four hours. I would like nothing more than to get out of here and get on with my life. Things got even better – Lisa, Brian, and Sydney came to see me. Sydney asked me how I was doing. I told her I was improving every day, and that I might be able to go home tomorrow.

"That is fantastic news," she replied.

Then Lisa told me I looked so much better, and that being at home would accelerate my recovery. I said I had no doubt about that because I would have the best caregiver in the world – your mom.

"Yes, she is the best, all right."

Just then Sydney hopped up on the end of my bed. Lisa told her to watch out for all the tubing lines. Sydney said she would be careful and that she just wanted to be close to me and make me better. (She has always been good medicine for me.) I asked if they could stay until six because that would be when Elaine arrived. But Lisa said no, they had to go.

I told her I was so glad they had visited, and that I already felt better as a result.

Then they left and Sydney said as they walked out the door, "Feel better, Poppy."

When Judy came to take me for a walk a little later, I was totally energized. I told her, "We're going for two laps today." After they had detached me from all the various devices, we took off down the hall.

Judy said, "Slow down, Mr. Andretti. We are not timing this lap."

"Oh, you must have forgotten your calendar," I replied.

She laughed and told me she wanted me to be in one piece when they released me.

I made it all the way around the hall before I had to stop and rest. Then, I finished another lap, thinking, *All right, I'm ready for the outside world.* We returned to the room, and they hooked me back up once again.

Elaine came to see me around six. When I told her I might be released the next day, she jumped straight up in the air with her arms raised. (She looked like a high school cheerleader.)

"I can't believe it. I'm so happy!" she said.

We talked all night about what our life would be like with me at home again, and how grateful we were that I was alive. She left at nine thirty and I waited for her text, which came an hour later: "Night-night. Love you."

Then I called nurse Kay for my sleeping pill.

Homeward Bound

It was Monday, and Rachael was exceptionally cheerful that morning. She came in at seven thirty to tell me that I could go home. (*Yeah!*) She still had to administer my medications, though. I asked her if she could detach me so I could pack and she said as soon as Dr. Carman signed the release papers. "Now would not be soon enough for me," I told her.

Dr. Carman came in a little while later to confirm that I was going to be released. He also said I would have to return in eight or nine days so he could remove my abdominal drain, and again in five weeks to remove the stent. I asked how long it would be before I could be released. He said the staff had a procedure to follow for my release and it will probably take about an hour. He told me I was doing fine, and he would see me in eight or nine days.

Finally, about one thirty, Rachael showed up with a hospital administrator. They had me sign endless release papers and gave me the remainder of my medications, along with instructions on how to take them. When Elaine arrived, they gave her instructions on how to take care of me at home, and especially how to empty the neoprene bag attached to my stomach drain. Also, they explained that a home nursing service would be contacting us and would be taking care of me at home for another week.

Then they put me in a wheelchair and took me to the pick-up area by the parking lot. As I left the hospital and went out into the Southern California sunshine, I could feel myself choking up. It almost overwhelmed me, because it seemed like it had been forever since I had been outside. I was so grateful to be alive and able to smell the fresh air.

The nurse's aide helped me into the car, and we were on our way. When we arrived at home, Elaine had to help me into the house because I was not able to walk by myself. I was still wobbly. She guided me right to my favorite lounge chair. (Hallelujah!) Soon I was sitting in the chair that I had been dreaming about for the past twelve days.

Elaine made a simple dinner that night: salmon, rice, and spinach. I am here to tell you that it tasted so great after all the hospital food. It was my first homemade meal in nearly two weeks. After dinner I was so exhausted, I fell asleep in my chair. Elaine woke me up at nine thirty to go to bed. That was interesting because we had to climb two flights of stairs to reach our bedroom. With her supporting my body all the way, we finally made it. As I rolled into bed, I thought about the hospital bed I had been in and felt so grateful to be in my bed. There's nothing like your own bed, is there?

Then my mind went back to the hospital stay and my NDE. I still did not know my purpose. I did know that real estate was not my life's purpose, the universe showed me that by ripping it away from me. There was no market anymore for homes. The housing market had collapsed, and my health collapsed with it. I thought, *I don't have the energy anymore. I don't know why I'm here.*

*Your purpose in life is to find your purpose and
give your whole heart and soul to it.*
~ Gautama Buddha

Chapter 5:
Re-entry

It was Tuesday, my first full day at home, and I could not believe I slept in until ten o'clock. Elaine was waiting to help me down the stairs. After breakfast, I settled into my lounge chair again. As I looked around, I realized everything looked new to me, as if I were seeing it for the first time. It's like I really had died and come back to life. Now I had to take advantage of my second chance. So I started thinking, *I want to know. I want to go deeper into why I'm here and what my purpose is.* Because I received the message during my NDE, I knew I had to go on this journey. So I decided to start the meditation process.

When the nurse arrived (her name was Sally she took my vital signs and hooked me up to an IV. After ninety minutes, she removed the IV line from my arm and headed for the door.

"See you tomorrow," she said.

We went to bed early that night because I was very tired. Unfortunately, I had a bad night. I woke about every ninety minutes, drenched in sweat. Elaine had to change the sheets twice, and I changed my pajamas three times. I was uncomfortable, consumed with hot flashes and body aches. I remember thinking, I felt better in the hospital bed, but I was not going to let this get to me. I was so glad to be home. As I was lying there in bed, I thought, *I will get through this, plus I will still be at home.*

I woke up Wednesday, feeling much better and eager to start the day. Sally showed up at one-thirty the next afternoon. After hooking me up, she started the antibiotic drip. I told her what happened the previous night and asked why it had happened. She said that sometimes high doses of antibiotics could adversely affect the body, and to let her know if it happened again.

Searching for Meaning

After Sally left, I was feeling better, so I decided to try and make sense of what had happened to me the hospital. I had been studying different meditation techniques, including the Question and Answer technique, which is what I used that day.

I sat in a chair in a very quiet room and tried to clear my mind. I discovered that it is not easy and apparently takes a lot of practice. I started meditating and asked the question, "*What is my real purpose?*" and listened for an answer. After thirty minutes, I had no answer, so I stopped meditating. Maybe tomorrow.

So I thought back to my NDE and started thinking about energy and matter. Then I opened a book about Albert Einstein. Einstein's theory was $E=MC^2$. That is Energy = Mass times the Speed of Light squared. Mass is a coherent body of matter. So, he is saying matter and energy are two different forms of the same thing. If that's so, the experience I had with a supernatural being probably wasn't in matter; it was in energy. I don't think I could have reached out and touched that being. Since matter and energy are the same, then maybe life and death are the same. Maybe life is what we see, what our physical eyes and our brain can construct. And, we can't conceive of what we don't see, life becoming energy and living on forever after our body dies, even though it actually does.

Elaine broke the spell when she came over to empty my pouch, and told me dinner was ready. I noticed that I was really looking forward to meal time, unlike in the hospital.

I was a little apprehensive about going to bed, so I took a sleeping pill. What a difference a day makes. I slept all night. I was so happy. (So was Elaine.)

On Thursday, after breakfast, I decided to go for a little walk. Dr. Carmen had said I needed to exercise. So, with Elaine by my side, I walked to the end of our cul-de-sac and back. I was so excited to do that and to be outside in the fresh air.

After Sally had finished administering my IV, I decided to try meditating again. I went back to my quiet room, sat in a chair, and tried to clear my mind. Various thoughts kept popping into my head, which made it difficult to concentrate. I'm used to getting results, so I was becoming frustrated. But something told me to keep trying, so I did. Again, I asked, *What is my purpose?* After thirty minutes, nothing had come to me, so I decided to wait and try again the next day.

I was really looking forward to dinner. Elaine was going to prepare chicken on the barbecue, with corn on the cob. Doesn't that sound great? It was. That night, I went to bed early and slept like a log.

Oh No! Back to the E.R.

On Friday, we had the usual routine: early breakfast and lunch on the patio. It was a beautiful day in Southern California, and I was eagerly awaiting the arrival of nurse Sally, totally unaware of what was about to happen.

When Sally arrived, she took my vitals and then retook my blood pressure. I asked her if something was wrong. She told me my blood pressure was 90/50, and she was very concerned. She called the doctor, who told her to get me to the E.R. as fast as possible.

Here we go again.

Elaine drove me to the hospital. On the way, all kinds of thoughts were running through my head: *What is wrong? Am I going to die?* Then I thought, *No, I am not going to die, I have not yet fulfilled my purpose.* I suddenly felt very calm and peaceful.

When we arrived at the hospital, they put me into one of the emergency room cubicles, and we awaited the emergency room doctor. When he arrived, he looked at me and said, "I reviewed your chart; you don't need to be alarmed. This is quite common with patients in your condition. We should have you stabilized and be able to release you in two to three hours."

What a relief!

After they had hooked me up to an IV, I asked the nurse what was in it. She told me it was fluids and some medication to control my blood pressure and that I would feel better in no time.

Finally, after three and a half hours, I was released, and we headed home. When we got back to the house, I was more determined than ever to find my purpose. This time, I had to meditate in my lounge chair because I was worn out from my E.R. visit. I tried to clear my mind and asked, *What is my purpose?* I was getting better at keeping my mind clear of any thoughts.

Even though no answer came to me, I was pleased with my progress.

Elaine made my favorite dinner that night: linguini and meat sauce with turkey meat.

I was in heaven. Again, I slept well that night, probably because I was exhausted from my visit to the E.R.

Success! Purpose Revealed

It was Saturday, back to normal – a regular day. Breakfast early and lunch on the patio.

After lunch, I went for a walk. With Elaine at my side, we walked to the end of our cul-de-sac and back, just like before. I was again exhilarated to be outside and upright.

After Sally had completed my IV, I was pretty alert, so I went back to the quiet room to meditate. I closed my eyes, cleared my mind, and asked the Universe, *What is my purpose?* After a few minutes, I experienced a powerful revelation:

"*I must share my experience with as many people in the world as possible and show them how to live a better life.*"

Wow! My mind was racing. I was so excited.

How do I do this? Where do I start?

When I calmed down, I started to think logically.

How can I reach thousands of people all over the world?

The answer became obvious: a book. I would write

a book to document my experience, and everyone in the world would have access to it through Amazon and bookstores. But first, I must recover my health, so I made that my top priority. I knew I was going to see Dr. Carman in two days, and would ask him what I needed to do to effect a fast recovery.

I no longer wanted to tell people how they could have temporary joy through owning a home. This time, I wanted to tell them that they could have joy whether they owned a home, rented, or were sleeping in a forest, because, even though their body could disappear tomorrow, they could make someone else's life better today.

I went to bed that night completely confident that my life plan was in place.

Sunday was my final day of home nursing; the next day I would see Dr. Carman. All was well. Before Sally arrived, I went for my daily walk. With Elaine's help, we went down to the park, two blocks away, and back. A little further than the day before.

Sally finished administering my last IV and told me to take oral antibiotics for another three weeks. I thanked her for all her help as she left.

I was now confident in my recovery because I had a mission to accomplish. My thoughts were all very positive, and I was excited to start my new journey.

That night I had a hard time going to sleep because

my head was buzzing with ideas about how I was going to accomplish my mission.

Drained Out

It was Monday, and we were going back to Dr. Carman to have my abdominal drain removed. Yeah! Another milestone.

After he had removed the drain, he said, "Come back in five weeks so we can remove the stent. It will require surgery, but you can go home the same day. My surgery scheduler will set it up for you."

Now was my chance, so I asked, "What do I need to do speed up my recovery?"

"First, take your antibiotics for the next three weeks. Then, eat healthily and try to get some form of exercise, but don't push yourself. Take the multivitamin they gave you at the hospital and stay away from sick people; you are still in a weakened condition. Call me if you have any problem. Otherwise, I will see you in five weeks."

We left for home with a prescription for getting well.

It had been five weeks since Dr. Carman had removed my abdominal drain. A lot had happened during that time, including surgery for a malignant mole on my left thigh.

I had also finished the course of those terrible antibiotics that were taking a toll on my stomach.

It was now time to see Dr. Carman again, so we went back to the hospital. They put me into a room to prep me for surgery. The nurses spent the next sixty minutes getting me ready. Finally, the operating room staff came for me. It was my sixth surgery in just sixty days

I knew the operating room well: stark white and squeaky clean with a temperature of the North Pole. Dr. Carman was there to greet me.

"Hello, Mr. Steinhoff, this won't take long. You'll be back home in no time."

"I certainly hope so. Don't I need the stent any longer?"

"No, you don't. We have to remove it to prevent any complications."

As the anesthesiologist approached, I looked around the room. I felt right at home. I saw lots of electronic equipment and scopes to protect me. Dr. Carman, two nurses, an assistant, and, of course, the anesthesiologist, all this just for me, imagine that?

I was totally at ease.

Then, the anesthesiologist said, "It's time." He gave me what he called the "good stuff."

I went out like a light. When I awoke, I was back in my room with a nurse at my side.

She asked me how I felt. I told her I felt fine and asked if I could go home. She said they needed to stabilize me first and it should take thirty to forty-five minutes.

Dr. Carman then arrived.

He said, "Everything went well. You have no more bile leaks. You can go home now. Follow your instructions and call me if you have a problem."

After I got dressed, the nurse brought Elaine in and told her to meet us at the pick-up area with her car. They put me in a wheelchair and then took me down to the first floor and outside to our car. I was thrilled to be out of the hospital. Again, I would have jumped for joy if I could have.

We then went home to start our new life – one with purpose.

Don't die with your music still in you.
~ Dr. Wayne Dyer

Chapter 6: Reboot Your Life

When I found my purpose and stopped living Off-Purpose, I knew I didn't want to see another soul living Off-Purpose. That's when I decided to share my story in the book you're reading. My purpose was not just to tell my story; it was to help people think and embody the question: If I died today, am I On-Purpose?

Now I want to go deeper with you in a process that will help you flesh out the thoughts and beliefs that are holding you back from living the life you are meant to live, a life On-Purpose. I'm going to present you with a series of provocative, introspective questions about different aspects of your life, and help you discover what you really want, help you heal your past, and help you feel a sense of excitement for your future. Then, when you pass, you will have no regrets, plus you'll have a sense of peace and fulfillment.

You may not have answers for all of the questions below right now, but stay the course; the answers will eventually come to you.

It is my desire that this exercise will cause you to have a breakthrough and find your true calling, so you can begin to live your life On-Purpose.

> *We should be ashamed to die until we have made some major contribution to mankind.*
> ~ Horace Mann

Life Inventory

Take this inventory of your life and answer the following questions as honestly as you can. It is important for your future and for finding your life's purpose.

Death

We're all going to die. No one will get out of this life alive. The question is, what happens next?

Is there life after death? Each religion treats the subject somewhat differently, but almost all of them believe in some form of afterlife.

Deepak Chopra says that after death, your soul leaves your body and ascends to one of many astral planes. Your soul will go to the plane that corresponds closest to the vibration frequency of your former life.

Quite different from the Christian belief that your soul goes to either heaven or hell after you pass.

DEATH

1. **If this were your last breath, would you feel comfortable dying?**

Are you afraid of dying? If you have lived your life On-Purpose, you will have no regrets and feel peaceful about going.

DEATH

2. What scares you the most about death?

Is it that you don't want your life to be over because you still have unfinished business? Being On-Purpose means you have no unresolved issues when you're ready to leave this world.

DEATH

3. Do you believe in life after death?

Almost six billion people on this planet do believe in it. Are you one of those? If you are, you are probably living On-Purpose and are truly ready for the next life.

DEATH

4. What happens when your body dies?

Most people believe their soul survives the death of their body and transcends into a new reality. But, there are many who say that after death, our soul is transformed into a new state: it becomes energy. We have no eyes, but we can still see. We can be everywhere at once; there are no limitations. There is no beginning, and there is no end. It is difficult for us to wrap our minds around this concept.

In Hinduism, they believe that a person's current life is an intermediate step in a long procession of lives. In other words, reincarnation. When your body dies, your soul will be put into a new body. When you are reborn, you bring along the talents you've developed from all previous lives. They believe, for example, that Mozart was able to compose symphonies at a very early age can because he brought along his talents from previous lives.

There are many ideas about what form your soul will take, but it will be in heaven if you live a purposeful life.

God

Eighty-four percent of the world's population is involved in some form of organized religion. That's almost six billion people. With that many people, there must be something to this, right?

The major religions are Christianity, 32 percent (2.2 billion); Islam, 23 percent (1.6 billion); Hindu, 15 percent (1 billion); and Buddhist, 7 percent (500 million).

Monotheism accounts for 55 percent of the population. This includes the Christianity and Muslim faiths. In monotheism, they believe God is the supreme being, and they only worship him. They consider God to be omnipotent(all-powerful), omnipresent (all present), and omnibenevolent (all loving.)

Where do you fit in?

GOD

1. Do you believe in a supreme being?

If you do, you are not alone. Nearly four billion other people also do. If you are religious, then you probably believe you were put here for a specific purpose, and you need to find out what it is so you can live your life On-Purpose.

GOD

2. Do you believe you have a soul?

If you believe in God, then you know you have a soul, and your soul will survive after your body dies. This is a core belief of On-Purpose people.

GOD

3. **Do you feel supported by your spiritual community?**

It is essential that you are supported in your mission by like- minded people of your faith. This is important to your success as an On-Purpose person.

GOD

4. **Do you make time in your life for spiritual practice?**

Connecting with your spiritual community is essential for you.

Attending services and being actively involved in your religion is part of that.

You will do it naturally when you are On-Purpose.

Family

If you died today, how would your family deal with your death? Will they be at peace with it, or will they have unresolved issues with you?

Is there anything you still wanted to do with, or for, your family?

Anything you still wanted to say to them?

Do you need to apologize to your adult daughter, for example, for not supporting her decision to open a dress shop and ignore her degree in accounting? Or, maybe you always wanted to take your family on a cruise.

On-Purpose people make sure all these things are settled long before they pass.

FAMILY

1. What have you always wanted to do with members of your family?

For example, you always wanted to take your family to Disneyworld, but keep putting off. What is holding you back? What are you waiting for?

When people are on their death bed, they don't say, "I wish I had worked more." They say, "I wish I had done more with my family."

If you are living On-Purpose, you will put your family first.

FAMILY

2. **Do you have any unresolved issues with any of your family members?**

It is important for you to handle these issues sooner, rather than later, so you don't have to deal with them on your death bed. Maybe you have an ongoing feud with your father about how you discipline your children. You need to resolve this issue so that it doesn't distract you from your mission.

FAMILY

3. **Are there things that need to be said to a member of your family?**

Do you need to tell your estranged daughter that you love her and are sorry you hurt her? Or, do you need to tell your spouse how much you love and appreciate her more often?

You need to handle these issues now, so they will not be a problem for you as your death approaches. If you are living your life On-Purpose, you will make sure everything is clear with family members.

FAMILY

4. **What have you always wanted to do for your family?**

Your family is your most important support group. Sometimes, it is good to do something unexpected for them just to show your appreciation.

For example, you could hire a local chef to come to your home and prepare a gourmet meal for your entire family, and give everyone in your family a day off from cooking. On-Purpose people always go the extra mile for their family to show their love and appreciation.

Health

Your health is vital to your existence. If you don't have good health, everything else is insignificant. You really need to take good care of your body so you can enjoy life. According to doctors, that includes eating a balanced diet, getting regular exercise, and reducing stress.

You know that when you are sick and have to miss your weekly golf game, you are not a happy camper. Plus, it is difficult to handle tasks vital to attaining your goals.

HEALTH

1. **Are you taking good care of the body you were entrusted with?**

This is the only body you get. It needs your undivided attention so you can remain healthy and able to do the things you love to do. If you want to make a difference, you need to make your health a top priority.

HEALTH

2. What is your daily exercise program?

It is important to have an effective physical regimen to enhance your health and ensure that you live longer. Being physically fit is essential, so you have the vitality to accomplish your purpose. Remember to check with your doctor before beginning any exercise program.

HEALTH

3. Does your current diet support a healthy lifestyle?

If not, get some professional advice about what you should be eating and drinking. Your doctor can be a key resource.

Once you are eating right, you will feel better, have more energy, and be able to do more. Being On-Purpose means giving your body the nutrition it needs.

HEALTH

4. How is your stress level?

Doctors tell us that excess stress is very bad for your health. It can cause things like high blood pressure, asthma, fatigue, and heart problems. Stress can also make existing problems worse like it did for me with asthma and acid reflux. People living On-Purpose take stress seriously and do everything they can to minimize it.

Business / Career

Do you love what you do?

Are you in the right career?

Do you get excited when you get up in the morning, and can hardly wait to get to work?

If not, you need to take a look at your life. Maybe you're not in the right profession. This exercise will help you to determine where you need to go with your career.

Also, do you have any money issues related to your business? Is there anyone you owe money to that should be repaid? For example, you borrowed $3,000 from a friend three years ago to fund an advertising campaign, and never paid it back. Take care of that now. Call your friend and tell him how you will pay him back. Don't leave it for your loved ones to handle after you are gone.

BUSINESS / CAREER

1. Do you love the work you are currently doing?

If you don't love what you are doing, you may be living Off-Purpose. It is paramount for you to find your purpose, and when you do, it will most likely be something you love to do.

BUSINESS / CAREER

2. **Do you feel your current profession is in alignment with your purpose in life?**

You should be doing something that aligns with your life's purpose. This will enhance your ability to accomplish your mission by allowing you to be more effective in helping others.

BUSINESS / CAREER

3. Does what you are currently doing benefit others?

Doing something that improves other people's lives is the most fulfilling and rewarding career you could have. That is what being On-Purpose is all about. Don't stop until you are there.

BUSINESS / CAREER

4. Do you owe money to anyone, or does anyone owe you money?

If you have money issues, is important to resolve them in a timely manner. You don't want to leave it for your loved ones to resolve after you are gone. People living On-Purpose make sure all money issues are handled before they pass.

Finances

If you died tomorrow, have you done everything you can to put your personal finances in order to ease the financial burden on your spouse and family after you are gone?

I'm positive most of you would want to make sure your loved ones were taken care of after you pass. You don't want them to have to scramble to unravel your financial situation. For example, if you leave $300,000 in 20 CD's in 20 different banks with no record anywhere, your loved ones will have great difficulty figuring it out. Do you really want that?

Also, make sure all your important financial documents are in one place, like a safety deposit box in your bank, and make sure your loved ones know where that place is.

FINANCES

1. Do you have an up-to-date will?

If you want to make it easier on your loved ones after you are gone, make sure you keep your will updated. Being On-Purpose means you take care of this so that your family does not have to deal with problems associated with your estate after you are gone.

FINANCES

2. Do you have a record of your insurance policies?

On-Purpose people do this so their loved ones don't have to search for this crucial information after they die. You want to ease their burden because they will already be stressed enough.

FINANCES

3. Do you have a list of your bank accounts, CD's, credit cards, retirement accounts, etc.?

Being On-Purpose means you are totally organized with your financial documents to make it easier on your loved ones when you pass.

Having all your documents in one place will help them enormously.

FINANCES

4. Do you have a list of your assets and liabilities?

This includes automobiles, real estate, and personal property, as well as auto loans, mortgages, and personal debt (including credit card debt).

Make sure your loved ones know where this list is located.

Understand that we have a complex reality and it is important to educate your loved ones about what they should do after you are gone. Having your financial house in order will be a big help. This is what On-Purpose people do for their loved ones.

Dreams / Desires

You should have a list of everything you want to do before you "Kick the Bucket."

What do you want to have, what do you want to do, and what do you want to be? You say, "I want to go to Tahiti; someday I will get there." Make that someday now, put it on the list. Write down everything you can think of, where you want to travel, places you want to visit, things you want to do, retirement savings amount, things you want to buy, classes you want to take, skills you want to learn, etc. Don't leave anything out. Your list should contain at least 100 items. Some people call this a "Bucket List." I call it a "Life Goals List."

Don't limit your thinking. For example, if you like golf and want to become a professional golfer, your goal should not be just to become a professional, it should be to win a major tournament. If you want to write a novel and turn it into a movie, your goal should not be just to make a movie; it should be to win an Oscar.

To give you an idea, my list includes taking magic lessons and performing at the Magic Castle in Los

Angeles, taking stand-up comedy lessons and appearing at the Improv, and, of course, winning an Oscar.

The question is: Why do you want these things and why aren't you doing them now? Your heart could stop tomorrow. Or today. What's really holding you back?

In addition to your Life Goals List, you need a "Chuck-it List." This is a list of things you're never going to do, or are going to stop doing because they are not important anymore when you're living your life On-Purpose. It can be things like stop wasting time and energy on tasks unrelated to your new purpose.

If you want some help, I have a free Bucket List Kit for you. There are instructions on how to obtain it at the end of this book.

DREAMS / DESIRES

1. What are your five greatest desires?

You should have a plan to make them happen. If you don't, it is just a wish list. On-Purpose people prioritize their dreams and take action to turn them into reality.

DREAMS / DESIRES

2. What is your greatest dream ?

What is the one thing that, more than anything else, will get you up in the morning and make it so you can't wait to start your day? If you know what it is, this could be your major purpose. On-Purpose people have one major desire, and it is their life's purpose.

DREAMS / DESIRES

3. **What is the one thing you could acquire that would make you jump for joy?**

Life is too short. Be happy. Do something nice for yourself, and acquire that one thing right now. You will be more productive because of your joy. On-Purpose people realize how important it is to be happy.

DREAMS / DESIRES

4. **What is on your chuck-it list?**

This list is as important as your bucket list of life goals. Don't take it lightly. Be sure to include everything you are going to stop doing and things you are never going to do because they don't relate to your life's purpose. On-Purpose people have this list to guide them and keep them on track.

Values

Your values determine who you are and what matters to you. To determine your values, you must first decide on your highest priorities. For example, if you had a free afternoon, what would you do?

Would you play golf or have lunch with your sister? Decisions like these reflect your values.

Defining your core values will allow you to do more of the right things and enjoy life more.

VALUES

1. What are your core values?

Appendix A consists of a comprehensive list of values. You can use this list as a guide to determine which values are important to you. Look it over and see which ones call out to you and feel a part of you. Living On-Purpose means living your core values.

VALUES

2. Do you use your core values to determine how you use your time?

One of your most important assets is your time. You have only a finite amount of time to live, so you must use it wisely. Let your core values guide you in how you spend your precious time. Using your values to prioritize your time will serve you well in becoming On-Purpose.

VALUES

3. Do you make decisions based on your core values?

Being clear on your values will make it easier to make decisions. You always choose the way that is compatible with your values. That makes decision-making much less complicated. On-Purpose people always decide in favor of their core values.

VALUES

4. Do you take action based on your core values?

When you are ready to take action on any task, adhering to your values will keep you on the right path. Your actions will reflect your values and your life's purpose.

Goals

If you want to achieve anything in life, you must have goals. The goals have to be realistic, achievable, and measurable. Otherwise, they're just wishes. You can have goals for all areas of your life: Family, Financial, Business, Spiritual, Social, and Personal.

Prioritizing your goals becomes much easier when you are clear on your core values. You can measure each goal against your values to determine if it is in alignment.

GOALS

1. Have you set goals for yourself?

Having goals is critical to achieving anything you want to accomplish. Otherwise, you just have a wish list. Living On-Purpose is having a set of goals to achieve each day (and beyond).

GOALS

2. Do you work toward achieving your goals?

If you want to be On-Purpose, you must set a course of action that will allow you to attain your goals, and follow that course to the letter.

GOALS

3. Are the goals you have right now in alignment with your values?

You must do this to be effective in reaching your goals. Living On-Purpose means prioritizing your goals to align with your values.

GOALS

4. How are your goals doing for you?

You need a system to measure the effectiveness of your actions and how well they are serving your mission. Being On-Purpose means tracking how well you are doing in achieving your purpose.

Mental

As you probably know, having a sharp mind is essential for almost everything you do in life. It affects your job, your family, your community involvement, even your health.

There are many ways you can stay mentally fit. You can keep a journal, work on puzzles like Sudoku, read books, or take classes. I use an online program to improve my memory.

Equally important is getting enough sleep. It is essential for maintaining a fully functioning brain.

Another thing that is very important is your mental attitude. You have to maintain a positive mental attitude (PMA) to be happy and succeed at anything. This is easier said than done in our environment, but you need to work on it continually. If you do, you will see positive results in all areas of your life.

MENTAL

1. Do you maintain a positive mental attitude most of the time?

Living On-Purpose is being aware of your attitude from moment to moment, and changing it from negative to positive as needed.

MENTAL

2. How do you keep your mind sharp?

Neuroscientists say that one way to accomplish this is by doing something entirely foreign to you, like using your left hand to eat when you are right handed. On-Purpose people are constantly improving their minds with challenges like puzzles, classes, and online programs.

MENTAL

3. Make sure you get enough sleep.

Having enough sleep will allow your brain to operate at full capacity.

On-Purpose people make getting enough sleep a priority, even if they have to take occasional naps.

MENTAL

4. Are you good at managing your time?

Being On-Purpose means you are in total control of your time. You do not have time to waste on tasks unrelated to your purpose.

On-Purpose people always utilize some type of time management program.

Personal Growth

This is an area often neglected by a lot of people. They become settled in their comfort zone and are hesitant to leave it. Personal growth is essential to moving forward in your career, as well as in your private life.

When you are setting goals for personal improvement, focus on what you want, not what you don't want.

Improving your knowledge by reading or taking classes will enhance your career, as will community involvement.

PERSONAL GROWTH

1. Which areas of your life need improvement?

There are certain skills and abilities that are critical to achieving your mission. Being On-Purpose means you know what they are and are committed to improving them.

PERSONAL GROWTH

2. **What are you doing today to improve in critical aspects of your life?**

You should know where you need improvement, and concentrate on enhancing those areas. Being On-Purpose means you are constantly working on ways to improve your performance.

PERSONAL GROWTH

3. Are you committed to improving yourself?

Without your commitment, improvement will be difficult or impossible. You must be totally committed to self-improvement to facilitate achieving your life's purpose.

PERSONAL GROWTH

4. Why do you want to improve?

It is important to know the reason why you are taking the time and making the effort to improve your skills. On-Purpose people always know what they need to improve upon, and why they need to do it. It is usually because they need that skill to complete their mission.

Social

There are a lot of relationships in your life in addition to your family. There are your close friends, your social friends, your coworkers or employees, your community friends, and your church or synagogue friends. If you have children, you have friends who are parents of your children's friends. The list goes on.

That's a lot of relationships to maintain. With that many, things are bound to go wrong somewhere. You want to resolve these issues in a timely manner because you don't want to feel regret when you are on your death bed.

Better to do it now rather than waiting until it is too late.

SOCIAL

1. **What have you wanted to do for a friend, but have never found the time for?**

For example, your best friend loves the opera, but can't go because they have a young child they don't want to leave with a babysitter. You can offer to babysit for them and maybe even buy their tickets. On-Purpose people are always there for their friends.

SOCIAL

2. Are there any issues with friends that need to be resolved?

If you have unresolved issues with a friend, you should do whatever you can to make it right. On-Purpose people do this so they can pass in peace with no regrets.

SOCIAL

3. **Are there things you wish you could do with friends, but are held back for some reason?**

Maybe you want to spend the week in Las Vegas with your friends but are held back because of the expense. Well, it's not that you don't have the money, you are just using it for something else. This is a matter of priorities. If you want to be On-Purpose, you need to have established priorities.

SOCIAL

4. Are there any relationships in your life you would like to explore further?

Perhaps you met someone at your child's soccer game who you might want to become better friends with because you have a lot in common. You should reach out to them. On-Purpose people always like to expand their social circle.

Community

Being involved in your community has a lot of rewards. You have the feeling of belonging, but more importantly, you have a sense of fulfillment because you give back to the community.

Contributions can be monetary, in-kind, or volunteering your time. You should decide where you want to put your resources. It might be your place of worship or a worthy nonprofit that you relate to. Whatever you decide, make your presence known. Show the organization that you are sincere and want to help.

You will also make friends, plus, as I found, it can be good for business. I joined the local chamber of commerce and became involved immediately. They appointed me chairman of the membership committee. I found that people wanted to work with me because they saw my commitment to the chamber. I sold a lot of real estate over the years because of that.

Believe me; you receive more in return than you will ever give.

COMMUNITY

1. **Are you currently connecting with your community?**

If not, you should seriously consider it. There are many rewards, and you will find it fulfilling. Giving back to your community is part of being On-Purpose.

COMMUNITY

2. Have you determined what form your involvement will take?

You can contribute money, in-kind support, or your time. Whichever you choose, your community will be grateful, and you will feel good about it. People who are living On-Purpose thrive on this.

COMMUNITY

3. Are you taking a leadership role in your community?

Use your business skills to help a community organization attain its goals. This will give you a real sense of achievement. Taking the lead is a blueprint for On-Purpose people.

COMMUNITY

4. **Could your business provide in-kind support for a community group?**

This is a good way to become involved without using any of your hard-earned cash. Plus, you will most likely receive favorable publicity for your contribution. Your involvement is part of being On-Purpose.

Fun / Hobbies

It is important for your mental health to have something other than work to occupy your time. If you have any spare time, how do you occupy that time?

Having a hobby is one of the best things you can do for yourself. It should be something you really love to do. Time seems to just fly by when you're engaged in your favorite hobby.

You also need something to do just for fun. For me, this is performing magic tricks. For my wife, it is for us to frequently visit the "Happiest Place on Earth" (Disneyland).

Having these diversions is essential to balance your life and give you some perspective.

FUN / HOBBIES

1. What is your favorite thing to do in your spare time?

(If you don't have spare time, create some!) You really need to incorporate something you love to do into your daily schedule for your mental well-being. Being On-Purpose means making this a daily priority.

FUN / HOBBIES

2. What are your hobbies?

Hobbies should be an important part of your life. If you love things like oil painting or golfing, pursue it with all your might. You never know, you might even find your life's purpose in your hobby. On-Purpose people have creative hobbies to pursue.

FUN / HOBBIES

3. What do you do for fun?

Remember fun? Life is too short not to enjoy it. You need to incorporate fun things into your busy schedule because you will be more effective in living a purposeful life.

FUN / HOBBIES

4. Do you take personal time for yourself?

This is a big one. Too many people are caught up in the daily demands of their lives and don't take time for themselves. On-Purpose people always schedule some personal time each week.

Reconciliation

Reconciliation is defined as restoration of friendly relations.

I first had to reconcile with myself. I was angry with myself for allowing my body to get run down and loosing my sense of purpose. So I had to reconcile that with myself. Then, I had to reconcile the situation I had generated for my wife, knowing I had created fear, struggle, and suffering for her. Even though Elaine would never think this way, I still needed to reconcile this with myself.

While I was still in the hospital, I thought about my brother. I had an estranged brother, Tom. We didn't get along and rarely talked even though he lived just ninety miles away. I didn't want to die without reconciling our relationship.

One day I received a call from a friend of Tom's. He said Tom was in the hospital, and it looked serious. Not giving it a second thought, Elaine and I got in the car and drove to Palm Springs. When we went into his room at the hospital, I locked eyes with Tom and saw a very frightened person. He started to cry.

"I don't want to die," he said.

Right then, our differences seemed petty, so I went over and gave him a hug.

He started sobbing and said, "I am so sorry. I love you, and I want to be close again."

I told him I loved him too, and that we were close again, and that I would always be there for him. After we left Tom, we talked to his doctor, who told us he had a terminal brain tumor and did not have long to live.

We were devastated.

He died four months later, and he passed in peace because we had reconciled. I was holding his hand when he passed. That is the power of reconciliation.

If you have someone you should reconcile with, don't wait, do it now.

RECONCILIATION

1. **Are there people in your life you have issues with that you would like to resolve?**

I am sure there are some. If you are living On-Purpose, you will talk with these people and resolve the issues before you are on your death bed.

RECONCILIATION

2. Are you in conflict with someone who is dying?

Maybe it's your father, and you need to tell him you love him and are sorry for everything before he passes. On-Purpose people take care of these things before it's too late.

RECONCILIATION

3. How will you resolve these issues?

You might need to write to someone to clear the air. She may not accept your olive branch, but, you can still say, *"I reached out and gave it my best shot. I told her I loved her and I told her I'm sorry."* That is what you do if you want to be On-Purpose.

RECONCILIATION

4. Are you motivated to resolve your people issues?

You should be, because when you do, you will feel free and liberated. Plus, you won't have to die with that issue burning inside you. You'll have no regrets. But it won't work unless you make it a priority. This is essential for your success in being On-Purpose.

Redemption

In the religious sense, redemption is the forgiveness of your sins so you can enter heaven. This is the belief of most organized religions. There is a feeling that before your soul leaves this world, you want to feel a sense of redemption.

Otherwise, redemption is defined as atoning for a mistake.

In my industry, it is defined as paying off a mortgage, clearing a debt. There are things we need to clear, things we don't want to leave behind when we pass. It's similar to making amends to someone you hurt.

I think back to when the nurses were walking me down the hall in the hospital, and my mind was flooded with this feeling that if I died, what unfinished business would I leave behind? What would I regret not doing?

Have you ever regretted doing something for which you would like forgiveness? The deepest issue for most people, I think, is the regret of how you handled things in the past and the people you have hurt.

When I was forty, my father and his second wife were about to have dinner when they realized they were out of butter. They got in their car and started for the store, six blocks away.

They never made it. A young kid who was drunk ran a stop sign and broadsided their car. My father was killed instantly. His wife was badly injured but survived. The driver received a sentence of life in prison and had to live with the fact he had killed someone and changed their family's life forever. Worse than being in prison, he was imprisoned in his heart and mind.

About ten years later, he wrote to my stepmother to ask for forgiveness. She went to the prison to meet him and give him that forgiveness. They hugged, and both started to cry.

Redemption is a powerful thing, isn't it?

For me, it was hard to look back at my involvement in the whole real estate feeding frenzy and realize I should have done more for those people who were underwater. My book had solutions for them. I should have made sure it reached more people. But now, it is too late. The moment has passed. I do ask for their forgiveness, though.

Ask for forgiveness now. Don't wait until it is too late.

REDEMPTION

1. **Have you done things in your life you regret and for which you want forgiveness?**

I think we all do. On-Purpose people are different from most because they identify these issues and take action to rectify them.

REDEMPTION

2. What action do you need to take to make amends?

Maybe you humiliated someone at work and need to apologize for your actions. Being On-Purpose means you seek redemption for your negative actions that have hurt other people.

REDEMPTION

3. How will you redeem your self?

For example, maybe you obtained a lucrative contract by exaggerating your competition's faults. You need to make amends to your competitor by asking for forgiveness. On-Purpose people always have a plan for seeking forgiveness.

REDEMPTION

4. Is forgiveness for your misdeeds important to you?

Redemption will never happen for you unless you make it a priority. Then you will seek forgiveness. This is what On-Purpose people do.

Don't die with your music still in you.
~ Dr. Wayne Dyer

Your Purpose

You don't have to have an NDE to discover your purpose. You can ask yourself, "Am I doing what I love and loving what I do?" Does it bring you joy? Are you excited to get up every morning and start your day?

If not, think about your life right now. How would you change it? What are your big dreams? If you don't know the answers, ask for guidance. I used meditation. Try it. Ask for guidance and see what happens. You can also use prayer if you're religious. Have you ever had a "feeling" that you should do something? Your soul is always trying to guide your life. It is constantly sending messages to you in many ways (for example, through the words of others in lyrics of songs, or through newspaper articles or signs on the road). Pay attention and trust your inner voice. You may have a revelation like I did.

Plus, you may live longer. Researcher Dan Buettner, who studied communities with high concentrations of

100-year-olds, found that one of the factors these people shared in common was a strong sense of purpose. In one of these communities, Okinawa, they call it "Ikigai," which translates to "Why I wake up in the morning."

His research revealed that knowing your purpose can add as much as seven years to your life expectancy.

Finally, when you are On-Purpose, you are in the flow. Life seems effortless, and opportunities just come to you. Everything just seems to fall into place.

You come alive and become unstoppable.

YOUR PURPOSE

1. **What do you love to do?**

Think about the times when you were doing something that made you really happy. What were you doing? If you always do what brings you the most joy, it will be much easier for you to live On-Purpose.

YOUR PURPOSE

2. What would you do if you had in infinite supply of money?

Most people's dreams are hindered by the lack of money. But, if you didn't have to worry about money, what would you do? On-Purpose people don't think about where the money will come from to fund their dream. They find their calling first, then figure out a way to fund it.

YOUR PURPOSE

3. What are you uniquely good at doing?

Think about what you are good at, that most people are not. It will usually be something you love to do. On-Purpose people most often do what comes easy to them and what they're really good at doing.

YOUR PURPOSE

4. **If you could succeed at whatever you choose, what would you do?**

If success were guaranteed no matter what you did, what would you really do? This will probably be your life's purpose. On-Purpose people usually succeed because they are doing what they love and are good at.

Carve your name on hearts, not tombstones.
Your legacy is etched into the minds of others
and the stories they share about you.
~ Shannon L. Adder

Legacy

Forget about yourself. Instead, concentrate on serving others. By giving back, you will experience the unparalleled joy of seeing how you have made a difference in their lives. Going through an NDE was a life-changing experience for me. Now, I really want to contribute to the greater good of the universe by improving people's lives. You always need to serve people in a way that makes YOU feel good. Also, you can create an income by doing something you love to do.

Steve Jobs' mission was to make a dent in the universe. Now, hundreds of millions of people around the world use innovative Apple products (it is estimated that the company has sold one billion i-Phones worldwide). His legacy lives on in all those people.

Walt Disney was a legend. His goal was to be the

world's top producer and provider of entertainment. Now there are Disneyland and Disneyworld parks all over the world. What a legacy!

Perhaps this book won't be the next War and Peace, but if people read it and it changes their lives for the better, I will have achieved my purpose. My legacy will live on in those people. You can do the same.

It doesn't have to be something big, like building Disneylands.

You could write a book. When it is published, your book will exist forever. You will become immortal.

In our regional performing arts center, you can dedicate a seat in the main theater with a donation. A brass plate with your name engraved on it will be placed on that seat permanently. Also, your donation, along with many others, will make it possible for thousands of people to attend future performances in the years to come.

I did a little more than that. In addition to being a member of the fundraising committee to build the local performing arts center (we raised over $200 million),

I personally donated more than $40,000. My name is on a plaque, along with many others, on a wall inside the center. Every time I attend a performance there, I go look at it. As I stand there, staring at my name, I think about how much pleasure our center has brought, and will bring, to so many people, and knowing this gets me all choked up,

Not everyone can build theme parks all over the world, but you can still make a difference in your world. When you fulfill your Purpose, you will leave a legacy in all the people you have touched. You will become immortal.

LEGACY

1. What do you want to be remembered for?

Determining what this is might have a bearing on what your major Purpose could be, or it could be the result of living your life On-Purpose.

LEGACY

2. Who will remember you and why?

Think about all those who will be impacted by you when you fulfill your mission. People will remember you when you change their lives for the better.

LEGACY

3. **What can you leave behind to improve the lives of others?**

Consider this. The results of your mission will have touched the lives of many people, and it will live on in those people. What you leave behind will be a direct result of living your life On-Purpose. Your legacy will continue long after you are gone.

LEGACY

4. **What will your epitaph say?**

Have you never thought about this? Most people don't. But, living your life On-Purpose will impact a lot of lives and create plenty of material for your epitaph.

Off You Go

Now that you have discovered a lot of information about yourself, use it to help find your higher calling.

It's similar to real estate, when you want to obtain the highest value for a piece of land; you have to change the zoning to its highest and best use.

Use the answers to the questions in the previous section to change your "zoning" and to determine your "Highest and Best Use": your life's purpose.

Then, organize your life around it. There will be no stopping you.

Your greatest self has been waiting your whole life, don't make it wait any longer.

~ Steve Maraboli

Epilogue

I've always wanted to make a difference. My whole fascination with NASA and going into space was to know that the human species could become more and more intelligent and enriched as it explores new frontiers. (Already, we have GPS software, LED's, flat screen TV's, cordless tools, solar energy for homes, laptops, memory foam, and much more as a result of space program technology.) And, I became involved in real estate because I thought I could help people fulfill their dream of homeownership.

But then, the whole real estate market came crashing down and my health came crashing down with it.

I found myself in the hospital, and I slipped out of this world. That's when a supernatural being showed me there is life after death and that I had a greater purpose. What is that purpose?

I discovered that my purpose was to share my story with others so they can experience less fear of death and realize how important each moment is in their life and why they should live On-Purpose.

Now that you have completed the journey with me and taken inventory of your life, it is my wish that you find your true calling and start living your life On-Purpose today. Don't wait any longer

Remember, you really *can* experience extraordinary happiness, fulfillment, and contentment. You really *can* feel alive and live life to its fullest. You really *can* make a difference and leave a legacy. Plus, you really can live longer to do it.

As a bonus for you, here are some tips I picked up in life:

Life Tip #1: *You Need to Visualize a Relaxing, Safe Place Where You Can Go When You Need to Escape Reality.*

Life Tip #2: *When You're Faced With Adversity. You Always Need Someone Who Will Be Your Rock.*

Life Tip #3: Don't Ever, Ever Let a Negative Outcome Come Into Your Head. Don't Even Let Your Mind Go There.

Life Tip #4: Your Family is Your Most Important Asset. Cherish Them.

Life Tip #5: No Matter How Much Life Throws at You, Don't Let it Get to You. You Can Overcome Anything.

I hope my book has inspired you to take action. Best wishes for your success.

H. Richard Steinhoff
http://www.hrichardsteinhoff.com/

P.S. If you liked my book, please go to www.amazon.com/books and leave a review.

About the Author

H. Richard Steinhoff is an author, speaker, and community leader dedicated to improving people's lives.

His community involvement has included serving as vice-president and director of the Chamber of Commerce; president of Center 500 (a major fundraising organization for the Segerstrom Center for the Arts in Orange County); ex-officio director of the Segerstrom Center for the Arts; director of the Laguna

Niguel Community Council; president of The Club at Rancho Niguel; president of the Crown Royale Homeowner's Association; as well as being a member of the Chancellor's Club of the University of California, the Irvine Exchange Club, and the California State University Alumni Association.

His real estate background includes serving as president of the ERA Broker Council, president of the Broker Council of Southern California, vice-president and director of the Board of Realtors, director of the California Association of Realtors, as well as membership in the National Association of Realtors.

Richard has been a featured guest on talk radio shows in cities that include Cleveland; New Orleans; Chicago; Baltimore; Charlotte; Phoenix; and many in California, New York, and Florida; along with several television news programs, including two appearances on Fox Evening News in Los Angeles.

He has received the *Man of the Year* Award from the Irvine Chamber of Commerce, the *President's Award* from the Muscular Dystrophy Association, and has been listed in *"Who's Who in California"* as well as *"Who's Who in the West."* He was made an *Honorary Member for Life* by the California Association of Realtors. He has also recently received a *Certificate of Recognition for Community Leadership* from the California State

Legislature.

His education includes a Bachelor of Science degree in Business Administration from California State University and a Certificate in Industrial Relations from the UCLA Graduate School of Business.

Richard is also a member of the American Mensa Society.

Bonus Gift

As a thank you for purchasing this book, H. Richard Steinhoff is offering you the following FREE gift:

- **Bucket List Kit**

    - Everything you need to finally complete your list of things you want to do before you die. The kit includes:

        1. Forms

        2. Instructions

        3. An example of a completed list with suggestions

    To claim your free gift, go to:
    http://goo.gl/VqxEaF

Appendix A: List of Values

1. Abundance
2. Acceptance
3. Accessibility
4. Accomplishment
5. Accountability
6. Accuracy
7. Achievement
8. Acknowledgement
9. Activeness
10. Adaptability
11. Adoration
12. Adroitness
13. Advancement
14. Adventure
15. Affection
16. Affluence
17. Aggressiveness
18. Agility
19. Alertness
20. Altruism
21. Amazement
22. Ambition
23. Amusement
24. Anticipation
25. Appreciation
26. Approachability
27. Approval
28. Art
29. Articulacy
30. Artistry
31. Assertiveness
32. Assurance
33. Attentiveness
34. Attractiveness
35. Audacity
36. Availability
37. Awareness
38. Awe
39. Balance
40. Beauty
41. Being the best
42. Belonging
43. Benevolence
44. Bliss
45. Boldness
46. Bravery

47.	Brilliance	77.	Confidence
48.	Buoyancy	78.	Conformity
49.	Calmness	79.	Congruency
50.	Camaraderie	80.	Connection
51.	Candor	81.	Consciousness
52.	Capability	82.	Conservation
53.	Care	83.	Consistency
54.	Carefulness	84.	Contentment
55.	Celebrity	85.	Continuity
56.	Certainty	86.	Contribution
57.	Challenge	87.	Control
58.	Change	88.	Conviction
59.	Charity	89.	Conviviality
60.	Charm	90.	Coolness
61.	Chastity	91.	Cooperation
62.	Cheerfulness	92.	Cordiality
63.	Clarity	93.	Correctness
64.	Cleanliness	94.	Country
65.	Clear-mindedness	95.	Courage
66.	Cleverness	96.	Courtesy
67.	Closeness	97.	Craftiness
68.	Comfort	98.	Creativity
69.	Commitment	99.	Credibility
70.	Community	100.	Cunning
71.	Compassion	101.	Curiosity
72.	Competence	102.	Daring
73.	Competition	103.	Decisiveness
74.	Completion	104.	Decorum
75.	Composure	105.	Deference
76.	Concentration	106.	Delight

107. Dependability
108. Depth
109. Desire
110. Determination
111. Devotion
112. Devoutness
113. Dexterity
114. Dignity
115. Diligence
116. Direction
117. Directness
118. Discipline
119. Discovery
120. Discretion
121. Diversity
122. Dominance
123. Dreaming
124. Drive
125. Duty
126. Dynamism
127. Eagerness
128. Ease
129. Economy
130. Ecstasy
131. Education
132. Effectiveness
133. Efficiency
134. Elation
135. Elegance
136. Empathy
137. Encouragement
138. Endurance
139. Energy
140. Enjoyment
141. Entertainment
142. Enthusiasm
143. Environmentalism
144. Ethics
145. Euphoria
146. Excellence
147. Excitement
148. Exhilaration
149. Expectancy
150. Expediency
151. Experience
152. Expertise
153. Exploration
154. Expressiveness
155. Extravagance
156. Extroversion
157. Exuberance
158. Fairness
159. Faith
160. Fame
161. Family
162. Fascination
163. Fashion
164. Fearlessness
165. Ferocity
166. Fidelity

167. Fierceness
168. Financial independence
169. Firmness
170. Fitness
171. Flexibility
172. Flow
173. Fluency
174. Focus
175. Fortitude
176. Frankness
177. Freedom
178. Friendliness
179. Friendship
180. Frugality
181. Fun
182. Gallantry
183. Generosity
184. Gentility
185. Giving
186. Grace
187. Gratitude
188. Gregariousness
189. Growth
190. Guidance
191. Happiness
192. Harmony
193. Health
194. Heart
195. Helpfulness
196. Heroism
197. Holiness
198. Honesty
199. Honor
200. Hopefulness
201. Hospitality
202. Humility
203. Humor
204. Hygiene
205. Imagination
206. Impact
207. Impartiality
208. Independence
209. Individuality
210. Industry
211. Influence
212. Ingenuity
213. Inquisitiveness
214. Insightfulness
215. Inspiration
216. Integrity
217. Intellect
218. Intelligence
219. Intensity
220. Intimacy
221. Intrepidness
222. Introspection
223. Introversion
224. Intuition
225. Intuitiveness
226. Inventiveness

227. Investing
228. Involvement
229. Joy
230. Judiciousness
231. Justice
232. Keenness
233. Kindness
234. Knowledge
235. Leadership
236. Learning
237. Liberation
238. Liberty
239. Lightness
240. Liveliness
241. Logic
242. Longevity
243. Love
244. Loyalty
245. Majesty
246. Making a difference
247. Marriage
248. Mastery
249. Maturity
250. Meaning
251. Meekness
252. Mellowness
253. Meticulousness
254. Mindfulness
255. Modesty
256. Motivation
257. Mysteriousness
258. Nature
259. Neatness
260. Nerve
261. Nonconformity
262. Obedience
263. Open-mindedness
264. Openness
265. Optimism
266. Order
267. Organization
268. Originality
269. Outdoors
270. Outlandishness
271. Outrageousness
272. Partnership
273. Patience
274. Passion
275. Peace
276. Perceptiveness
277. Perfection
278. Perkiness
279. Perseverance
280. Persistence
281. Persuasiveness
282. Philanthropy
283. Piety
284. Playfulness
285. Pleasantness
286. Pleasure

287. Poise
288. Polish
289. Popularity
290. Potency
291. Power
292. Practicality
293. Pragmatism
294. Precision
295. Preparedness
296. Presence
297. Pride
298. Privacy
299. Proactivity
300. Professionalism
301. Prosperity
302. Prudence
303. Punctuality
304. Purity
305. Rationality
306. Realism
307. Reason
308. Reasonableness
309. Recognition
310. Recreation
311. Refinement
312. Reflection
313. Relaxation
314. Reliability
315. Relief
316. Religiousness
317. Reputation
318. Resilience
319. Resolution
320. Resolve
321. Resourcefulness
322. Respect
323. Responsibility
324. Rest
325. Restraint
326. Reverence
327. Richness
328. Rigor
329. Sacredness
330. Sacrifice
331. Sagacity
332. Saintliness
333. Sanguinity
334. Satisfaction
335. Science
336. Security
337. Self-control
338. Selflessness
339. Self-reliance
340. Self-respect
341. Sensitivity
342. Sensuality
343. Serenity
344. Service
345. Sexiness
346. Sexuality

347. Sharing
348. Shrewdness
349. Significance
350. Silence
351. Silliness
352. Simplicity
353. Sincerity
354. Skillfulness
355. Solidarity
356. Solitude
357. Sophistication
358. Soundness
359. Speed
360. Spirit
361. Spirituality
362. Spontaneity
363. Spunk
364. Stability
365. Status
366. Stealth
367. Stillness
368. Strength
369. Structure
370. Success
371. Support
372. Supremacy
373. Surprise
374. Sympathy
375. Synergy
376. Teaching

377. Teamwork
378. Temperance
379. Thankfulness
380. Thoroughness
381. Thoughtfulness
382. Thrift
383. Tidiness
384. Timeliness
385. Traditionalism
386. Tranquility
387. Transcendence
388. Trust
389. Trustworthiness
390. Truth
391. Understanding
392. Unflappability
393. Uniqueness
394. Unity
395. Usefulness
396. Utility
397. Valor
398. Variety
399. Victory
400. Vigor
401. Virtue
402. Vision
403. Vitality
404. Vivacity
405. Volunteering
406. Warmheartedness

407. Warmth
408. Watchfulness
409. Wealth
410. Willfulness
411. Willingness
412. Winning
413. Wisdom

414. Wittiness
415. Wonder
416. Worthiness
417. Youthfulness
418. Zeal

www.ingramcontent.com/pod-product-compliance
Lightning Source LLC
Chambersburg PA
CBHW052022070526
44584CB00016B/1860